When Money Triggers the Inner Child

When Money Triggers the Inner Child

Matthew Petchinsky

1

When Money Triggers the Inner Child

By: Matthew Petchinsky

Disclaimer

This book is a creative, educational, and reflective exploration of **inner child work through the lens of financial trauma**. It is designed to help readers understand how early emotional experiences can shape beliefs, behaviors, and reactions related to money, self-worth, and security. The practices, reflections, and ideas within these pages are intended for **self-discovery, emotional awareness, and personal growth**.

This book **does not constitute professional mental health, financial, or medical advice**. It is **not intended to diagnose, treat, cure, or prevent** any psychological or psychiatric condition. Readers experiencing significant distress, trauma symptoms, or emotional dysregulation are strongly encouraged to seek support from a **licensed therapist, counselor, or mental health professional** who specializes in trauma-informed care or financial therapy.

All exercises, visualizations, and reflective prompts should be approached **gently and at your own pace**. Financial trauma can evoke intense emotions tied to past experiences of scarcity, shame, or fear. If at any point the material feels overwhelming, readers are advised to pause, ground themselves, and return when ready—or process the emotions with a trusted professional.

While rooted in genuine psychological and metaphysical reflection, this book represents **one author's interpretation of healing through symbolic, emotional, and introspective frameworks**. It is not a substitute for therapy, crisis intervention, or financial counseling.

By reading this book, you acknowledge responsibility for your own wellbeing and agree to use the material as a **personal tool for insight and empowerment**, not as a replacement for professional support or clinical guidance.

Introduction

The child in you remembers.

They remember the sound of overdue notices sliding under a door, the tension in a parent's voice when bills came due, the hollow pit in the stomach when food was scarce, or the laughter of others when your clothes, toys, or dreams didn't match theirs. The adult you learned to work harder, to earn more, to survive—but deep inside, the child still trembles whenever money feels uncertain. That small voice hasn't vanished; it has only grown quieter, buried beneath responsibilities, debts, and the illusion of maturity.

Money, for many, isn't just numbers—it's **memory**. It carries the weight of past survival and the echo of unmet needs. Every spending choice, every savings goal, every financial panic can be traced back to a moment when your nervous system learned what danger felt like. When a parent's silence meant something terrible had happened. When the lights went out. When the rent notice came. When "we can't afford that" felt like a judgment of your worth rather than a financial limit.

This book is an invitation to **revisit those moments, not to relive them—but to rewrite them**. To walk back through the doors your inner child never felt safe behind. To sit beside them and say, "You did nothing wrong." You survived what you were never meant to endure, and the fears that haunt your bank account are not signs of weakness—they are **evidence of your body remembering what it took to stay alive**.

Through this journey, we will explore how the **nervous system, attachment patterns, and emotional safety** intertwine with financial decision-making. You will learn how scarcity is not always about how much money you have, but how safe you feel having it. You'll uncover why sudden success may trigger guilt, why saving can feel impossible, or why spending can feel like rebellion or relief.

Each chapter blends **inner child healing, shadow work, and financial self-inquiry**—three layers of the same transformation. You will be asked not to budget, but to **befriend**; not to plan, but to **soothe**; not to control, but to **witness** the scared parts of yourself that once associated money with survival, shame, or powerlessness.

At the end of each chapter, you will find:

- **Six Shadow Work Journal Prompts** designed to expose subconscious beliefs about safety, worth, and wealth.
- A **Guided Visualization** to gently reconnect with your inner child during moments of fear or scarcity.
- A **Meditation Practice** to ground your energy and integrate new emotional patterns around abundance and trust.

By the end of this book, your goal is not to erase the past—it's to **reparent the one who lived it**. When the inner child finally feels safe, your relationship with money transforms from reaction to creation. Decisions that once came from panic begin to flow from peace.

The work ahead is deep, emotional, and sacred. There may be tears, memories, or resistance. That is healing speaking. As you continue, remember: the child in you is not broken—they are waiting. It's time to take their hand, sit beside them, and whisper what no one ever said when you needed it most:

"You're safe now. I've got you. And together, we'll learn that money doesn't have to mean fear anymore."

Chapter 1: Meeting the Money-Wounded Inner Child

Before you can heal your relationship with money, you must first meet the part of you who *learned* what money meant. Beneath your current income, spending habits, and fears lives a child who once witnessed scarcity, instability, or emotional neglect connected to survival. That child isn't gone—they whisper every time you feel panic over a bill, guilt for wanting more, or shame for asking for help. This first chapter is where you meet them, not as a concept, but as a living memory carried inside your nervous system.

The Echo of the First Scarcity

Every financial behavior has an emotional ancestor. Perhaps you remember being told, "We can't afford that," or watching your parents fight over money late at night. Maybe you grew up in wealth but learned love was conditional upon success. Or perhaps your household never spoke about finances at all, leaving you in a fog of confusion and guilt when you started earning your own income.

Those early experiences *taught* your body what safety or danger felt like in relation to money. The moment money became a symbol of rejection, neglect, or unworthiness, your inner child began forming beliefs that still live within you:

- "If I have money, I'll lose it."
- "If I ask for help, I'll be punished."
- "If I'm not perfect, I'll be poor."
- "I must earn love by overworking."

These are not logical ideas—they are emotional imprints. They formed before you could understand economics, credit, or income. They were shaped by tone, by atmosphere, by the tension in a room.

Understanding the Money-Wounded Child

The "money-wounded inner child" is the version of you that associates financial uncertainty with emotional danger. When you face a financial decision today—spending, saving, investing—this child reacts first, often in panic, shame, or avoidance.

- If you freeze when checking your balance, it's the child protecting you from bad news.
- If you overspend for comfort, it's the child trying to soothe loneliness or fear.
- If you under-spend or hoard, it's the child clutching safety as if it could disappear at any moment.

To meet this child, you must look beyond adult reasoning and into *somatic memory*: how your body feels when you think about money. Do you tense your jaw? Does your stomach tighten? Do you feel dizzy, angry, small? The child speaks through those sensations.

Exercise: Writing the First Memory

Close your eyes and ask yourself, *What is my earliest memory involving money?*

Don't judge what appears. Maybe it's a piggy bank, a parent crying, a shopping trip, or being told you couldn't have something you loved. Write the scene in detail—the smells, sounds, emotions, and especially what the younger you *believed* in that moment.

Now read it back, imagining that child sitting across from you. What do they need to hear that they never heard then? What would safety have sounded like?

Visualization: Meeting the Child Beneath the Numbers

1. **Find a quiet space.** Sit or lie down comfortably. Close your eyes and take slow, deep breaths.
2. **Imagine a door labeled "Money Memories."** Behind it lies a room filled with gentle golden light.
3. As you open the door, you see your younger self. Notice their age, posture, and expression. They might be holding something—a bill, a toy, a coin, or nothing at all.
4. Sit beside them. Don't correct or teach. Just *listen.* Ask, "What do you remember about money?" Allow whatever emotions surface.
5. When they finish, place your hand over your heart and whisper: *"You don't have to protect me anymore. I'm here to protect you now."*
6. Visualize light surrounding both of you, sealing safety into that connection.

This visualization awakens the bond between your adult self (the provider) and the child self (the rememberer). It is the foundation of financial reparenting.

Meditation: Breathing Safety into Scarcity

Purpose: To calm the nervous system and teach the body that safety can exist even when uncertainty does.

1. Sit upright with one hand on your heart and one on your abdomen.
2. Inhale through the nose for **four seconds**, hold for **two**, exhale slowly for **six**.
3. As you breathe, silently repeat:
   "I am safe now. The fear is old."
   "I am learning to trust the present."
4. With each exhale, imagine releasing old panic stored in your body.
5. Continue for five minutes. When finished, thank your inner child for staying alive through difficult times.

Six Shadow Work Journal Prompts

1. **Memory Trigger:** When I think of "money," what childhood memory surfaces first, and what emotion comes with it?
2. **Inherited Fear:** What financial beliefs did I absorb from caregivers that still shape my adult behavior?
3. **Safety Illusion:** In what situations do I feel unsafe or small around money, and what does that remind me of from childhood?
4. **Emotional Substitutes:** How do I use spending, saving, or avoidance to recreate or numb childhood feelings?
5. **Reparenting Voice:** If I could speak to my younger self about money, what would I tell them now?
6. **Body Memory:** Where in my body do I feel money stress, and what might that part of me need to feel safe again?

Closing Reflection

You cannot fix what you have not met. This chapter was not about changing your spending habits—it was about acknowledging the *child who learned them*. Healing begins when compassion replaces shame.

As you move forward, remember: you are not weak for having emotional reactions to money—you are *remembering*. And every act of gentle attention is one step closer to rewriting the nervous system's definition of safety.

Chapter 2: How Scarcity Becomes Identity — And How to Unlearn the Belief That Worth Must Always Be Earned Through Struggle

The Silent Contract of Struggle

At some point in childhood, many of us signed an invisible contract that said:

"I must struggle to deserve anything good."

We didn't sign it consciously, of course. It was written in how our caregivers spoke about money, how they modeled exhaustion as virtue, or how love only came after obedience, effort, or achievement. Some of us watched our parents break themselves to survive—and we learned that **pain equals worth**. Others were told directly or indirectly that leisure, pleasure, or rest were signs of laziness. Over time, these lessons solidified into a belief system:

- "I must always work hard or I'm failing."
- "Ease means I'm doing something wrong."
- "If I'm not struggling, I'm unsafe."
- "I have to prove my worth before I can be happy."

Scarcity isn't just a condition—it's an *identity*. It becomes the lens through which you interpret every opportunity, every paycheck, every moment of rest. When scarcity is part of who you think you are, abundance feels threatening, unearned, or temporary.

The Origins of the Scarcity Identity

Scarcity begins as an *external* experience—too little food, too few resources, too much instability—but it becomes *internalized* through repetition. The child who saw the power shut off or the fridge empty doesn't just remember the event; they absorb the *message beneath it*:

"There isn't enough for me."

"My needs are a burden."

"Safety can vanish without warning."

When that child grows up, these messages hide beneath adult logic. Even if you have plenty, you might still feel panic when spending, guilt when receiving, or fear when resting. The body still expects the lights to go out. The mind still prepares for loss.

This creates what psychologists call *chronic scarcity conditioning*: your nervous system becomes addicted to the adrenaline of survival. Calm feels suspicious. Rest feels wrong. You keep busy not because you want to, but because your body only recognizes exhaustion as safety.

How Scarcity Masks as Discipline

In adulthood, scarcity often disguises itself as responsibility. It whispers:

"I'm just being practical."

"I can't afford to relax."

"I'll rest when I've earned it."

But beneath those statements lies fear. You may equate struggle with control because, as a child, the only people who had power were those who worked or suffered enough to deserve it. This is how scarcity becomes moralized—how struggle becomes identity. You feel virtuous when exhausted, guilty when calm, and uneasy when life finally feels generous.

Yet true security doesn't come from control—it comes from **trust**.

Unlearning the scarcity identity means teaching your nervous system that safety does not require suffering. It means separating *effort* from *worth*. It means learning that abundance can coexist with humility, that ease is not the same as carelessness, and that your existence alone is reason enough to receive.

Exercise: Mapping the Scarcity Stories

Take out your journal. Draw two columns. On the left, list the money and worth-related phrases you heard growing up (for example: "Money doesn't grow on trees," "We can't afford that," "Hard work is the only way to succeed," "Rich people are greedy").

On the right, write how each phrase made you *feel*—not think. Did it make you feel scared? Small? Ashamed? Motivated? Angry?

When finished, look for patterns. These are your inherited scarcity codes—the stories that quietly instruct your adult self how to behave around success and rest.

You cannot release what you haven't named. Seeing these beliefs in writing transforms them from invisible rules into editable scripts.

Visualization: Rewriting the Contract of Worth

1. **Find a comfortable space.** Breathe deeply until your shoulders relax.
2. Visualize a large parchment paper before you—your childhood "contract" of struggle. It might say, *"I must earn love,"* or *"I can't rest until everything is perfect."*
3. Gently pick up a golden pen in your imagination.
4. Read the old words aloud in your mind, then say: *"This belief kept me safe when I was small, but I am safe now."*
5. Begin to rewrite the contract:
    - "My worth is not measured by exhaustion."
    - "I am allowed to rest, receive, and enjoy."
    - "Ease is not laziness—it is balance."
6. When done, sign your name and fold the parchment into light, watching it dissolve into your chest. Feel warmth spread across your body as new safety takes root.

This visualization gently tells the subconscious that the survival contract has expired.

Meditation: The Breath of Enough

Purpose: To retrain the nervous system to feel safety in stillness and sufficiency.

1. Sit or lie down comfortably.
2. Place one hand over your chest and one on your lower belly.
3. Inhale through your nose as you silently say, *"There is enough."*
4. Exhale through your mouth as you say, *"I am enough."*
5. Continue this rhythm for five minutes, noticing any resistance or disbelief. Don't fight it—just breathe through it.
6. With each repetition, allow your breath to become slower and your body to soften.

This meditation reprograms the body to associate safety with presence, not productivity.

Six Shadow Work Journal Prompts

1. **Inherited Beliefs:** What were you taught—verbally or silently—about hard work, success, and struggle?
2. **Emotional Attachment:** When I'm not struggling, what emotions arise (guilt, fear, boredom, emptiness)?
3. **Identity Question:** Who am I without my struggle story? What part of me resists letting it go?
4. **Embodied Scarcity:** How does my body feel when I rest, and what memories surface when I allow ease?
5. **Worth and Receiving:** What would change if I believed I was worthy of abundance without proving myself first?
6. **Redefining Virtue:** How can I redefine discipline, effort, and success to align with peace instead of pain?

Closing Reflection

You are not broken for feeling uneasy in abundance—you are conditioned. Scarcity once kept you alive; it made you resourceful, resilient, and alert. But it was never meant to be your identity.

As you unlearn the belief that worth must be earned through struggle, you begin to live from **inherent worth**, not **conditional worth**. You start to see money, work, and effort not as punishment or proof, but as creative energy you can wield freely.

Chapter 3: Revisiting the First Scarcity Memories

The Memory That Still Breathes

The first time you felt scarcity, something inside you changed. It may not have been dramatic—a single denied request, a fearful conversation about bills, a moment when your home didn't feel safe—but that experience left an invisible mark on your nervous system. It wasn't just about *money*; it was about *survival*.

The body remembers the tone of voices, the silence at the dinner table, the heaviness of adults pretending everything was fine. It remembers the chill of uncertainty—the feeling that the ground beneath you could vanish.

This chapter is about returning to that first moment—not to relive it, but to understand it. Because until you revisit your first scarcity memory with compassion, it continues to run your life from the shadows.

How the First Scarcity Imprint Forms

Children are emotional mirrors. When caregivers are anxious, overworked, or desperate, that energy imprints onto the child as an internal belief. Before the age of seven, the brain is highly absorbent—it learns through observation and emotion, not logic.

For instance:

- A child who saw their parent cry over unpaid bills might conclude, *"Money hurts the people I love."*
- A child who asked for something and was shamed for it might decide, *"My desires make me bad."*
- A child who overheard constant fighting about finances might internalize, *"Money causes chaos. I must keep quiet to be safe."*

Even if your family later stabilized financially, the emotional scar often remains. The adult version of you may still hesitate to ask for help, over-give to feel safe, or undercharge for your work. These behaviors are not weakness—they are survival reflexes written decades ago.

Memory Retrieval: Opening the Door Gently

When revisiting old wounds, gentleness is not optional—it is essential. Trauma is not healed by confrontation but by compassion. The goal is not to "fix" the past, but to allow the part of you that froze in fear to finally be seen and soothed.

Before beginning, create a safe environment:

- Dim the lights or light a candle.
- Sit somewhere you feel grounded and supported.
- Have water and a journal nearby.

Now, take several slow breaths. Imagine that your adult self—the one reading this book—is a guardian entering the past not as a victim, but as a witness.

Exercise: The First Scarcity Scene

1. Close your eyes and ask softly:
   "When was the first time I felt there wasn't enough?"
   Don't force a memory—let it surface naturally. It may come as a vivid scene, a sensation, or even a fragment of emotion.
2. Describe everything:
   - Where are you?
   - Who is present?
   - What emotions fill the room?
   - What does your body feel like?
3. As you write, imagine sitting beside your younger self. They don't need fixing—they need comfort. Ask them, *"What are you afraid of right now?"*
4. Listen. Then gently reply,
   "I understand why you felt unsafe. You didn't cause this. You deserved to feel secure."

You are rewriting memory through empathy, teaching your nervous system that the event is over—and that you survived.

Why These Memories Still Hold Power

Unprocessed scarcity memories act like emotional magnets. They attract similar situations until they are healed. This is why some people repeat cycles of financial instability, guilt, or self-sabotage—because the inner child is unconsciously seeking *familiar chaos*, not because they want it, but because it's what feels known.

When the first scarcity wound remains unresolved:

- You might chase money yet never feel satisfied.
- You may reject abundance because it feels untrustworthy.
- You might cling to financial control to avoid repeating past helplessness.

Revisiting these origins is the only way to end the cycle. Awareness dissolves repetition. Compassion rewires identity.

Visualization: The Safe Room of Enough

1. **Close your eyes** and take a deep breath in through your nose, exhaling slowly through your mouth.
2. Imagine walking down a hallway lined with closed doors. Each door represents a memory of scarcity.
3. One door glows softly—it's the first one. Approach it without fear. Place your hand on the knob and whisper, *"I am ready to understand."*
4. As you open it, you see your younger self inside—perhaps sitting alone, crying, or watching adults argue.
5. Enter the room and sit beside them. Don't rush to comfort. Simply be present. Let your adult warmth fill the space.
6. When the child looks up, tell them:
   "You were never the problem. You were a child in an unsafe moment. I'm here now."
7. Visualize a gentle light surrounding both of you, transforming the air into calm safety.
8. Slowly close the door, but know that inside, healing has begun.

This visualization helps your subconscious brain replace the original panic response with an image of safety and care.

Meditation: Releasing the Scarcity Echo
Purpose: To quiet the old story that "it will happen again."

1. Sit comfortably and place your hand over your heart.
2. Inhale slowly, imagining you are breathing in golden light.
3. Exhale, releasing gray smoke—representing old fear and inherited worry.
4. Silently repeat:
   "That was then. This is now."
   "I am safe in the present."
   "My needs can be met with ease."
5. Continue for several minutes, letting your breath become slower and deeper.
6. If emotions arise, let them move through you like waves. Do not analyze—just allow release.

With consistent practice, this meditation retrains the nervous system to feel safety in the present, even when scarcity memories surface.

Six Shadow Work Journal Prompts

1. **Root Event:** What is the first memory I have of not having enough—whether money, attention, or safety?
2. **Emotional Imprint:** What belief about myself was formed in that moment? (e.g., "I'm unworthy," "I must hide my needs," "I can't trust others.")
3. **Repetition Cycle:** How does this early belief still show up in my financial life today?
4. **Inherited Fear:** Whose fear did I absorb—my parents', grandparents', or society's—and how has it shaped my decisions?
5. **Inner Dialogue:** What does my inner child need to hear to finally feel safe about money and survival?
6. **New Narrative:** If I could rewrite that memory as a story of empowerment, what would the new ending be?

Closing Reflection

You cannot heal what you refuse to remember—but remembering does not mean reliving. It means bringing awareness and love into places that were once filled with confusion and fear.

By revisiting your first scarcity memories, you acknowledge that the emotions were real, that the pain was valid, and that it no longer defines you. The adult you are today can hold what the child once could not.

Scarcity once taught you to survive. But survival is not the same as living.

This chapter invites you to begin the transition—from remembering lack to embodying *enoughness*.

Chapter 4: How Financial Neglect Becomes Adult Panic

The Quiet Pain of What Never Came

Neglect is one of the most invisible forms of trauma—especially financial neglect. It often leaves no scars, no dramatic story, no clear moment to point to. It lives instead in what was *missing*: reassurance, consistency, guidance, or safety. For many, it meant growing up in a household where money was a ghost—always mentioned in whispers, always a source of tension, or simply never spoken of at all.

As children, we may not have understood what was happening, but we *felt* it. The electricity of fear, the unpredictability of comfort, the silence after a parent's stress. Our nervous systems learned to prepare for disaster even when everything seemed fine. And now, as adults, that same system misfires—causing panic over bills, shame around spending, or an unexplainable fear of checking your balance.

Financial neglect does not just create economic instability—it breeds *emotional hypervigilance*. The child who never felt secure grows into an adult who cannot relax, even when there's enough.

Defining Financial Neglect

Financial neglect occurs when a caregiver fails to meet a child's needs for safety, education, or emotional clarity around money. This can take many subtle forms:

- **Inconsistency:** Sometimes there was plenty, other times nothing—and no explanation why.
- **Emotional Absence:** Money struggles consumed the adults, leaving no space for reassurance or understanding.
- **Silencing:** You were told not to ask questions about finances, creating confusion and fear.
- **Emotional Substitution:** Gifts replaced affection, or deprivation replaced boundaries.
- **Survival Role Reversal:** You were expected to "understand," to be the responsible one, or to emotionally care for stressed parents.

Neglect isn't only about poverty—it's about *emotional absence during financial instability*. Even wealthy households can raise financially neglected children when emotional connection is replaced by performance or silence.

How Neglect Turns into Panic

When your childhood environment was uncertain, your body learned that survival depended on constant readiness. That readiness never turned off.

Here's how it shows up in adulthood:

- **Hypervigilance:** Checking accounts obsessively, fearing something will go wrong.
- **Avoidance:** Refusing to look at bills or emails because they trigger old panic.
- **Overcontrol:** Micromanaging every dollar, unable to trust that money will flow.
- **Freeze Response:** Shutting down completely when financial challenges arise.
- **Shame Loop:** Feeling guilty for struggling, even when circumstances are improving.

This is not "bad money management." It is *trauma physiology*. The body is reenacting what it learned long ago: that money equals danger, unpredictability, and emotional disconnection.

Recognizing the Pattern

Financial panic rarely comes from present reality—it comes from old fear. The rent may be paid, but your body doesn't believe it. The bank account may be stable, but your inner child still flinches when someone mentions "expenses."

Ask yourself:

- When I feel money panic, am I reacting to the present or to a memory of the past?
- Whose voice does my fear sound like? A parent? A teacher? The silence itself?
- What did I need to hear as a child that I never heard about safety, stability, or abundance?

By tracing your panic to its roots, you begin to separate *the event from the emotion*—allowing your adult self to take back control.

Exercise: Listening to the Panic

1. When financial anxiety rises, pause before reacting.
2. Sit quietly and say aloud: *"This feeling is old. Let's see where it comes from."*
3. Place your hand over your heart and notice the sensations—tightness, heat, restlessness.
4. Ask: *"What does this feeling remind me of?"*
5. Let your inner child respond without logic. Perhaps they'll say, *"We might lose everything,"* or *"No one will help us."*
6. Answer softly, *"That was then. I'm here now. I have resources, awareness, and choice."*

This exercise begins to retrain your brain: panic is not a command—it's a memory calling for comfort.

Visualization: The Inner Bank of Safety

1. **Close your eyes.** Imagine walking into a large, warm bank—not made of stone, but of light. The air hums with calm energy.
2. In the center, there's a vault labeled **"Safety."** It holds everything you once lacked—stability, reassurance, presence.
3. Open it. Inside are the versions of you from different ages, waiting for safety deposits of love and attention.
4. One by one, hand each child a gold coin that glows with warmth. Each coin represents *consistency*. Say, *"You will never be forgotten again."*
5. As the vault fills with light, breathe deeply and affirm:
   "I have enough now. I am enough now. I am safe to receive."

This visualization rebuilds the emotional association between money and safety.

Meditation: Calming the Alarm System

Purpose: To teach your body that present-day challenges are not childhood crises.

1. Sit comfortably and take a slow breath in through the nose for **4 seconds.**
2. Hold for **2 seconds**, then exhale through the mouth for **6 seconds.**
3. With each breath, repeat silently:
   "I am not in danger."
   "My finances do not define my safety."
   "I can make calm decisions."
4. Focus on the rhythm of your heart. Notice how it steadies as your breath deepens.
5. Visualize each exhale releasing old panic stored in your chest and stomach.

Repeat this meditation daily when facing financial triggers. It gradually lowers cortisol levels and rewires the brain to recognize calm as safety, not struggle.

Six Shadow Work Journal Prompts

1. **Defining Neglect:** What forms of financial neglect did I experience—emotional, practical, or both?
2. **Emotional Consequences:** How did those experiences teach me to fear or over-control money?
3. **Triggers:** What present-day situations reignite my childhood fear of being unsupported or unseen?
4. **Reparenting Needs:** What would I say or do for my younger self during those moments of neglect?
5. **Self-Sabotage:** How does panic shape my financial choices today—through avoidance, overwork, or impulsivity?
6. **New Safety Narrative:** What would it feel like to live as though safety and abundance are my birthright, not my reward?

Closing Reflection

Financial neglect may have left you believing that no one would show up for you—that you must always fend for yourself. But every time you pause, breathe, and soothe the panic instead of obeying it, you become the adult that neglected child never had.

Healing does not come from perfect financial control—it comes from emotional safety. When you begin to trust that you can handle challenges without collapse, panic loses its power.

Chapter 5: Rebuilding Safety in the Nervous System

The Body Keeps the Financial Score

When your body has lived through financial chaos, deprivation, or uncertainty, it begins to treat *money* the same way it treats *danger*. Your nervous system can't tell the difference between a late bill and a threat to survival. Both feel like emergency. Both activate the same response: heart racing, muscles tensing, stomach dropping, and the mind spiraling into panic or shutdown.

This chapter is about reprogramming the *body itself*—the part that learned scarcity as danger—so that safety becomes your new default. Healing financial trauma requires more than budgeting or mindset work. You have to teach your *nervous system* that it no longer lives in crisis.

The work ahead blends somatic awareness, breathwork, grounding techniques, and gentle self-parenting. You will learn how to make your body a place that *feels safe to earn, spend, and rest.*

Understanding the Trauma Loop

When the nervous system is dysregulated by chronic scarcity, it tends to cycle between three states:

1. **Fight:** You try to control every financial outcome—overworking, obsessing, micromanaging details.
2. **Flight:** You avoid finances entirely, distract yourself, or impulsively spend to escape anxiety.
3. **Freeze:** You feel paralyzed, unable to make decisions, overwhelmed by guilt or fear.

Each state is the body's way of saying: *"I don't feel safe."*

Rebuilding safety doesn't mean stopping these responses overnight—it means learning how to regulate them in real time. When you can meet financial stress with calm, your decisions shift from survival to clarity.

The Science of Financial Safety

Safety is not a mindset—it's a *physiological condition*. The vagus nerve, which connects the brain to the body, governs the parasympathetic response (the "rest and digest" state). When it's strong and regulated, your body knows how to return to calm after stress.

But when financial trauma is stored in your body, your vagus nerve can remain stuck in a state of alert. You may feel jumpy even when nothing is wrong, or exhausted after simple money-related tasks.

The good news: **you can retrain your nervous system.**

Through breath, gentle body movement, grounding rituals, and consistent self-reassurance, you can rebuild your body's sense of stability—creating a baseline of calm that money can't easily shake.

Exercise 1: The Grounding of Enough

1. **Sit comfortably.** Place your feet flat on the floor.
2. **Press your palms gently** against your thighs. Feel the connection between your body and the earth beneath you.
3. **Inhale deeply** through your nose for a count of four, imagining stability rising up from the ground.
4. **Exhale slowly** for a count of six, releasing tension and old panic.
5. As you breathe, repeat aloud:
   "I am supported. I am safe. I am held by the earth."
6. Continue for three to five minutes until your breathing slows and your body softens.

This simple grounding practice trains the nervous system to associate money thoughts with physical steadiness, not fear.

Exercise 2: Safe Touch for Regulation

Touch is a primal language of reassurance, and your body doesn't distinguish between external comfort and self-comfort. Try this:

- Place your right hand over your heart and your left hand over your stomach.
- Say softly, *"I am here for you."*
- Breathe in for four seconds, hold for two, exhale for six.
- Imagine your heartbeat syncing with a steady, calm rhythm—the rhythm of safety.

Over time, this builds new neural associations. Your body learns: *Money stress is not an emergency. I can self-soothe.*

Exercise 3: The Safety Sequence

This sequence combines movement and breath to signal to your body that it's safe to return to calm after financial triggers.

1. **Shake:** Stand and gently shake your hands, arms, and legs. This discharges trapped adrenaline.
2. **Stretch:** Roll your shoulders, circle your neck, stretch your spine upward.
3. **Ground:** Place one hand on your heart, one on your belly. Feel the warmth.
4. **Breathe:** Inhale deeply, then exhale through pursed lips with a slow sigh.
5. **Affirm:** Whisper:
   "I am not my past. I am safe in the present. I can make calm decisions."

Repeat this after opening a bill, checking your account, or having a financial conversation. You're re-teaching the body how to return to peace instead of panic.

Visualization: The Safe Harbor

1. Close your eyes. Imagine yourself standing at the edge of a vast ocean. The water represents your financial life—deep, mysterious, and sometimes turbulent.
2. You step into a small boat—a sturdy vessel named **Trust.**
3. With every inhale, imagine wind filling your sails with stability. With every exhale, feel your anxiety drift away.
4. You steer the boat toward a glowing harbor of golden light. This harbor is *Safety*. It always existed—you just forgot how to find it.
5. As you arrive, whisper:
   "I can navigate the waves. I am no longer lost."

This visualization strengthens your body's association between calm awareness and financial confidence.

Meditation: The Parasympathetic Reset

Purpose: To train your nervous system to return to rest more quickly after financial stress.

1. Sit upright or lie down. Place one hand over your heart.
2. Breathe in through your nose for **4 seconds**, hold for **4**, exhale for **8**.
3. As you exhale, silently repeat:
   "Safety is my new normal."
4. Focus on the warmth of your chest and imagine it spreading through your body like sunlight.
5. If your mind wanders to worries, gently say, *"We're safe now,"* and return to your breath.

Regular practice creates a new baseline of peace—your nervous system begins to expect calm, not chaos.

Six Shadow Work Journal Prompts

1. **Safety Inventory:** When do I feel most unsafe around money, and what does my body do in those moments?
2. **Body Awareness:** What physical sensations do I associate with financial fear or peace?
3. **Healing the Reflex:** When I catch myself spiraling, how can I pause and bring safety back to my body?
4. **Old Associations:** What childhood experiences taught me that money equals danger?
5. **New Association:** What would it feel like if my body trusted money as a neutral, stable energy?
6. **Repatterning:** What daily actions can remind my nervous system that I am not in crisis anymore?

Creating a Daily Nervous System Ritual

To rebuild safety, you must train consistency into your body's awareness. Small, repeated practices create regulation faster than rare intense effort. Try this daily ritual:

1. **Morning:** Breathe for one minute while repeating *"I am safe to receive."*
2. **Midday:** Check in with your body. Notice if tension is creeping in—stretch, shake, breathe.
3. **Evening:** Write one line of gratitude for a financial moment that felt calm, not dramatic.

These small acts build the foundation for financial stability because they strengthen your internal sense of control and peace.

Closing Reflection

Your financial peace begins in your nervous system—not your paycheck. When your body learns to feel safe, you make clearer choices, attract healthier opportunities, and stop reacting from fear.

Every breath, stretch, and act of self-soothing is a declaration that the era of financial panic is over. You no longer live in survival mode—you live in *self-trust*.

Chapter 6: Creating a Nurturing Budget Plan

Budgeting as Emotional Safety — Not Restriction

For many people with money trauma, the word *budget* feels like a cage. It reminds us of deprivation, punishment, or control. Budgets were what our parents argued about. Budgets were why we couldn't have what we wanted. Budgets became the symbol of "not enough."

But when you approach budgeting from a place of healing, it transforms from a restriction into *a boundary of care.* A **nurturing budget plan** is not about denial—it's about safety, clarity, and compassion. It is a map that tells your inner child, *"I will take care of you now."*

This chapter will teach you how to build a budget that reflects your emotional needs as much as your financial goals. It will show you how to integrate nervous system regulation, self-care, and pleasure into your financial structure—so that your money plan becomes a tool of nourishment, not self-punishment.

Why Traditional Budgeting Fails the Traumatized Mind

Traditional financial advice assumes neutrality. It says: *Spend less than you earn. Save for emergencies. Invest for the future.* While logical, this approach ignores one critical truth: **you are not just managing numbers—you are managing emotions.**

If your nervous system still equates money with danger, deprivation, or shame, a rigid plan can trigger rebellion or collapse. You may start strong and then abandon it, blaming yourself for "lack of discipline." In reality, your inner child is resisting what feels like punishment.

A nurturing budget works with your psychology, not against it. It provides structure *and* comfort. It honors both the adult who manages money and the child who needs to feel safe doing so.

Principle 1: Begin with Safety, Not Guilt

Before looking at income or expenses, establish emotional grounding.

1. Take three deep breaths and place a hand on your heart.
2. Say aloud:
   "This is not about control. This is about care."
3. Remember: you are building protection, not perfection.

You are not "fixing your finances"—you are **building safety into your daily life.**

Principle 2: Budget for Feelings, Not Just Figures

A sustainable budget includes *emotional categories.* Most people only track bills, rent, and food. A nurturing plan also tracks comfort, joy, and regulation.

Example categories might include:

- **Safety Fund:** Emergency savings reframed as emotional security—money that tells your inner child, *"We can handle surprises."*
- **Nourishment Fund:** Meals, rest, or therapy—investments that regulate your nervous system.
- **Joy Fund:** A small monthly amount dedicated to play, creativity, or sensory pleasure. This rewires your brain to associate money with safety and enjoyment, not deprivation.
- **Rest Fund:** Savings for days off, vacations, or intentional stillness. Rest must be budgeted, not treated as a luxury.

When you give emotional names to your categories, you create a relationship of empathy with your finances.

Principle 3: Use Gentle Percentages, Not Punitive Ones

Instead of rigid rules like "Save 20% or fail," create flexible ranges that reflect your current capacity. Trauma recovery requires compassion.

For example:

- 50–60% for essential needs (housing, utilities, groceries)
- 10–15% for safety savings
- 10% for joy and regulation
- 10–15% for growth (debt payments, investments, education)
- 5–10% for generosity or giving

If one month you cannot meet these percentages, **you haven't failed.** You've simply adjusted to life. This flexibility tells your nervous system, *"We adapt instead of panic."*

Principle 4: Bring the Inner Child into the Conversation

When making financial decisions, pause and ask:

"What does the child in me need to feel safe right now?"

Maybe they need to know the fridge will be full. Maybe they need something comforting like a candle or book. Or maybe they need reassurance that saving money doesn't mean scarcity—it means protection.

You can even write letters to your inner child while budgeting:

"I know you used to be afraid when there wasn't enough. But now we plan together. I promise I won't let you go without safety again."

Integrating this voice keeps your plan emotionally connected rather than cold and abstract.

Exercise 1: The Gentle Audit

Before you build your new budget, perform what I call *The Gentle Audit*.

1. Gather the last three months of spending statements.
2. Highlight anything that made you feel peaceful, regulated, or cared for.
3. Then highlight anything that triggered guilt, anxiety, or shame.
4. Ask:
    - What purchases met emotional needs in healthy ways?
    - Which ones were survival reactions (panic spending, avoidance, over-control)?
    - Where can I reallocate funds to align with emotional safety?

This audit transforms judgment into understanding. You're not "bad with money." You're *reacting from past conditioning.*

Exercise 2: The Sensory Spending Plan

1. Choose one sensory cue for each category—something that makes your body feel calm when you think of it.
    - Safety Fund = a warm blanket
    - Nourishment Fund = a comforting meal
    - Joy Fund = sunlight on your face
    - Rest Fund = ocean waves
2. Whenever you move money between categories, visualize or feel that sensory cue.
3. This rewires your brain to experience budgeting as *grounding*, not *restricting*.

Money becomes tangible comfort, not an abstract threat.

Visualization: The Garden of Stability

1. Close your eyes and imagine standing in a small garden. Each flowerbed represents a category of your budget.
2. You walk along and water each one: safety, nourishment, joy, rest, and growth.
3. Some flowers are larger; others are seedlings. But none are weeds—they all deserve care.
4. As you water them, say softly:
   "I am cultivating stability. I am nurturing my future."
5. Visualize your inner child sitting nearby, smiling as they watch the garden grow.

This imagery helps the subconscious accept that budgeting can be a loving, creative process.

Meditation: Breathing with Abundance
Purpose: To connect financial planning with nervous system calm.

1. Inhale through your nose for **four seconds**, thinking, *"Money flows in."*
2. Hold for **two seconds**, affirming, *"I am safe with what I receive."*
3. Exhale for **six seconds**, thinking, *"I release control and trust flow."*
4. Repeat this cycle for several minutes before budgeting sessions.

This creates a physiological anchor between money and relaxation, helping the mind associate financial planning with stability instead of stress.

Six Shadow Work Journal Prompts

1. **Emotional Reflection:** What past experiences made budgeting feel restrictive or shameful?
2. **Redefining Safety:** What does a "safe" budget look like for my inner child?
3. **Trust vs. Control:** Where am I trying to overcontrol money out of fear, and where can I trust myself more?
4. **Allowance for Joy:** How can I build joy and comfort directly into my spending plan?
5. **Healing the Narrative:** What would change if I saw my budget as a friend, not a judge?
6. **Commitment to Care:** How will I remind myself that budgeting is an act of self-love, not punishment?

Practical Structure Example: The Nurturing Budget Framework

Category	Purpose	Emotional Statement
Safety Fund	Emergency and savings	"I can handle surprises calmly."
Nourishment Fund	Food, therapy, health, rest	"My body and mind deserve care."
Joy Fund	Hobbies, small pleasures	"I am allowed to enjoy life now."
Rest Fund	Vacations, recovery days	"Rest is productive. Rest is safe."
Growth Fund	Debt payment, education, skills	"I invest in my own stability."
Generosity Fund	Helping others, community, giving	"I am connected to abundance."

Use this as a living document—something that evolves with your needs and emotions.

Closing Reflection

A nurturing budget plan is not about strict numbers; it's a spiritual act of care. It's the adult self telling the inner child, *"I will keep us safe now, and I will do it kindly."*

Through conscious structure and emotional awareness, your finances become a garden of safety—one you tend with compassion, not fear.

Chapter 7: How Forgiveness and Emotional Release Restore Your Earning Capacity

The Invisible Weight You've Been Carrying

Many people believe they're blocked from earning more because of poor habits, lack of opportunity, or bad timing. In truth, the deeper obstacle is often **unforgiven pain**—emotional residue that still clings to past financial experiences.

If you've ever said, "I don't deserve more," "I always mess up money," or "I can't be trusted with success," you're not lacking discipline—you're living under the emotional gravity of guilt and shame. These emotions contract your nervous system, close your creative channels, and restrict your ability to *receive.*

Money is energy. It responds to your state of openness. When you are burdened with resentment, anger, or regret about the past, your energy says, *"I can't trust flow."* Forgiveness, then, isn't a moral act—it's a **financial liberation practice.** It clears the emotional clutter that keeps abundance from entering your life.

The Financial Guilt Cycle

Every moment of financial failure—real or perceived—leaves a trace. You may still feel guilty for:

- Overspending when you were younger.
- Failing to save during hard times.
- Depending on others for support.
- Not being able to provide for loved ones.
- Losing jobs, homes, or stability.
- Making decisions that felt "irresponsible."

These memories sink into the subconscious as emotional contracts: *"I must pay for that mistake by never having peace again."*

But you've already paid—with sleepless nights, anxiety, and shame. The lesson is learned. The punishment no longer serves you.

When you forgive yourself, you dissolve the old contracts and reprogram your nervous system to believe, *"I can earn, receive, and expand without fear of punishment."*

Forgiveness as Nervous System Regulation

Forgiveness isn't about excusing the past—it's about regulating the body so it stops living in it. When you think about a financial failure and feel tightness in your chest, that's your body still bracing for impact. Your nervous system hasn't realized the event is over.

Forgiveness reintroduces *temporal clarity*: the past is the past. You are safe now.

It shifts your body from a state of vigilance to receptivity—from protecting to creating. Only then can new ideas, opportunities, and confidence flow in.

Exercise 1: The Financial Forgiveness Timeline

1. **Draw a timeline** of your financial life, from your earliest memory to now.
2. **Mark the painful moments:** job losses, debts, poor choices, or scarcity periods.
3. For each one, write:
    - What happened.
    - What belief I formed about myself because of it.
    - What emotion still lingers.
4. Now, one by one, place your hand over each entry and say:
   "I release you. I forgive myself for not knowing what I know now."

This act separates memory from identity—you stop being the "person who failed" and become the "person who learned."

Exercise 2: The Letter of Release

Write a letter to your past self during one of your worst financial moments.

Use this template:

"Dear Me,

I remember what you went through. The fear, the shame, the confusion. You thought you had ruined everything, but you were doing your best with what you had. I forgive you for the choices you made out of survival. I understand why you panicked, avoided, or overcompensated. You didn't fail—you adapted.

I no longer need to punish you. I release us both into peace. We are safe to earn again, safe to receive again, and safe to trust life.

With love,

[Your Name]"

When you read this aloud, your nervous system receives it as truth. The inner child finally hears the words they've needed for years: *"You're forgiven."*

Why Emotional Release Unlocks Earning Power

When guilt dominates your nervous system, it restricts your ability to create, ask, or claim. Forgiveness frees the energetic channels responsible for your sense of possibility.

Here's how it transforms your earning capacity:

1. **Increased Creativity:** Emotional openness allows you to perceive opportunities that were once invisible in the fog of self-criticism.
2. **Improved Confidence:** Forgiveness dissolves shame, so you can market your skills, negotiate pay, or accept recognition without fear.
3. **Energetic Expansion:** The moment you release resentment, your emotional frequency rises. Money gravitates toward peace, not panic.
4. **Healthier Risk-Taking:** With guilt gone, decisions are no longer made from desperation but from intuitive clarity.

Forgiveness literally **changes your vibrational signature**—and your outer world rearranges accordingly.

Visualization: The River of Release

1. Close your eyes and imagine standing beside a wide, flowing river. The water sparkles under the sun. This river represents *time.*
2. In your hands, you hold small stones engraved with words like "shame," "fear," "failure," "regret."
3. One by one, drop each stone into the water. Watch them sink, carried away forever.
4. Whisper each time:
   "I release this weight. I choose freedom."
5. As your hands grow lighter, feel energy returning to your body. Imagine golden light rising from the river and filling your heart.
6. Say aloud:
   "I forgive myself. I open to abundance."

Your subconscious accepts visual imagery more powerfully than logic. This ritual communicates release at a cellular level.

Meditation: Breathing in Forgiveness

Purpose: To physiologically release guilt and expand your receiving capacity.

1. Inhale deeply through your nose for **four seconds**, imagining warm, golden light entering your chest.
2. Hold for **two seconds**, saying inwardly: *"I am human. I am learning."*
3. Exhale slowly through your mouth for **six seconds**, releasing a cloud of gray mist—your body's stored guilt.
4. Repeat for at least five minutes, letting each breath deepen the feeling of peace.
5. When finished, place your hand on your heart and whisper:
   "I am forgiven. I am free to receive."

Over time, this meditation becomes a signal to your body that safety and abundance coexist.

Six Shadow Work Journal Prompts

1. **Unforgiven Moments:** What financial mistakes do I still hold against myself or others?
2. **Emotional Ownership:** What sensations arise in my body when I think about those events?
3. **Inherited Shame:** Whose guilt am I carrying that isn't mine—parents, partners, or ancestors?
4. **Release Statement:** What would forgiveness sound like if I spoke it aloud right now?
5. **Abundance Connection:** How does clinging to guilt block my creativity, receptivity, or success?
6. **Freedom Declaration:** What would it feel like to earn money without carrying any shame at all?

Exercise 3: Forgiving Others Who Mishandled Money

Sometimes, your scarcity wounds come from the actions or neglect of others—parents who mismanaged money, employers who underpaid, partners who betrayed financial trust. Forgiving them doesn't condone their actions; it liberates *you* from carrying their energy.

Try this visualization:

1. Picture the person standing across from you in a neutral, safe space.
2. Say silently: *"I release the hold your actions had on my peace."*
3. Visualize the energetic cord between you dissolving into light.
4. Feel your body lighten. That energy now belongs to you again—it can fuel creativity, work, and joy.

Forgiveness reclaims the energy that was trapped in resentment, redirecting it toward growth.

Exercise 4: The Receiving Practice

Now that forgiveness has cleared emotional clutter, you must retrain your body to feel safe *receiving.*

1. Each morning, say aloud:
   "I allow abundance to come to me easily."
2. Throughout the day, notice small moments of receiving—a smile, warmth, gratitude, or rest. Acknowledge them aloud: *"I received this."*
3. Your nervous system begins to associate receiving with safety, not danger.

When your body feels safe to receive, income and opportunity follow naturally.

Closing Reflection

Forgiveness is the bridge between financial fear and financial flow. You cannot create from a clenched heart. You cannot expand while gripping the past. Every act of release—every breath, every tear, every "I forgive you"—is an act of reclamation.

When you forgive yourself, you restore access to your **innate earning power**—the creative life force that fear once blocked. You begin to trust money again because you trust *yourself.*

Forgiveness is not a single moment; it is a practice of returning to wholeness. Each time you breathe through guilt, you are telling the universe, *"I am ready to receive."*

Chapter 8: The Alchemy of Play — How Creativity and Joy Reopen the Flow of Wealth

The Forgotten Currency of Joy

When survival has been your only language for years, *play* feels foreign—maybe even dangerous. Those who grew up with financial instability or emotional neglect learned early that safety came through control, not curiosity; through caution, not creativity.

But the truth is this: **play is the nervous system's proof of safety.** You can only play when you feel secure enough to relax. And without play, your ability to create, innovate, or earn collapses into repetition and fear.

In this chapter, we'll explore how reawakening play and creativity reconnects you to the natural abundance that trauma once shut down. You'll learn that joy is not frivolous—it's *functional.* It repairs the energy pathways that allow inspiration, opportunity, and prosperity to flow freely again.

Why Trauma Suppresses Play

A traumatized mind often equates play with irresponsibility. You may hear an internal voice say:

- "You don't have time for that."
- "You should be working."
- "Relaxing means you're lazy."

That voice isn't your truth—it's your *survival programming*. When you were a child, financial or emotional chaos made play unsafe. If your parents were stressed, laughing too loud might have drawn scolding. If you felt poor, wanting toys or fun seemed selfish. The nervous system learned: **play = danger of punishment or rejection.**

Now, as an adult, that same reflex blocks abundance. When life finally gives you space to breathe, you fill it with worry. You keep proving you're working hard enough instead of feeling safe enough to enjoy what you've built.

Healing begins when you remember: joy was never the problem—it was the *evidence of freedom* you weren't allowed to have.

Play as a Financial Regulation Tool

Play does what no budget or plan can: it repairs your relationship with trust. When you play—paint, dance, garden, write, build, experiment—your brain releases dopamine and oxytocin, the same chemicals linked to creativity, confidence, and connection. These neurochemicals regulate your stress response, making your body *biologically capable* of handling risk, opportunity, and growth.

You literally become better at earning when you're calm enough to innovate. Abundance doesn't emerge from tension—it blooms from safety, curiosity, and pleasure.

In short: when you play, your nervous system opens the door to new wealth.

Exercise 1: Remembering Your First Joy

1. Close your eyes and ask yourself: *"What did I love to do before I worried about being good at it?"*
2. Don't overthink—let the image arise. Maybe it's drawing, making up stories, running barefoot, or singing to no one.
3. Write that memory down in detail. Feel the texture of the joy: the smells, the sounds, the emotion.
4. Ask: *"When did I stop doing this? Who told me it wasn't important?"*
5. Now, reclaim it. Make a small plan to do this again in some form this week—not for success, not for outcome, but for *reconnection.*

You're not reviving a hobby—you're reviving a lifeline.

How Play Rebuilds Your Money Energy

Play restores three things that scarcity stole:

1. **Imagination** – the ability to see possibilities where fear sees walls.
2. **Permission** – the internal safety to try, fail, and try again without shame.
3. **Presence** – the focus to notice opportunities and synchronicities that rush past anxious minds.

When you play, the brain enters *theta state*—the same creative frequency associated with meditation and flow. In this state, new ideas and intuitive solutions surface effortlessly. You begin to see income streams, artistic ventures, or inspired decisions that your fear-blinded self could not perceive.

Visualization: The Workshop of Joy

1. **Close your eyes.** Imagine walking into a bright, sunlit workshop. Shelves are lined with paints, clay, instruments, notebooks, seeds—symbols of creative energy.
2. Your inner child sits at a table, working joyfully, surrounded by colors and laughter.
3. Walk toward them. Watch how easily they create without self-doubt.
4. Say softly: *"You are safe to play now. Nothing bad happens when you're happy."*
5. Join them—touch the paint, the tools, the laughter. Let your body absorb the memory of unrestrained creation.
6. As light fills the room, whisper: *"Joy is profitable. My creativity is safe to prosper."*

This visualization rewires your subconscious association between joy and danger, turning it into joy and safety.

Exercise 2: The Prosperity Play List

Create a "Prosperity Play List"—a list of playful, sensory activities that soothe and excite you. Include at least ten items, such as:

- Dancing barefoot for five minutes.
- Drawing with no purpose.
- Rearranging your workspace with candles or plants.
- Cooking a colorful meal while playing music.
- Journaling as if money were a living friend writing back.
- Taking a spontaneous walk without checking your phone.

Each act tells your nervous system, *"I am alive and unthreatened."* Over time, this lightness expands your emotional tolerance for success—you stop expecting wealth to bring pain.

Forgiveness and Play: The Twin Portals of Flow

Forgiveness (Chapter 7) clears space; play fills it with life. Forgiveness opens the door to abundance, but play invites abundance to *stay*.

When you allow yourself to play again, you're silently saying:

"I no longer live in survival. I trust joy enough to participate in it."

This trust sends a signal to your subconscious—and to life itself—that you are ready to receive without punishment.

Meditation: Breathing in Lighthearted Abundance
Purpose: To replace guilt with joy in the nervous system.

1. Sit comfortably and place a hand over your heart.
2. Inhale deeply through your nose for **four seconds**, imagining golden light entering your chest.
3. Exhale through your mouth for **six seconds**, smiling gently as you release old tension.
4. With each inhale, silently say: *"Joy fills me."*
5. With each exhale, say: *"Wealth flows through me easily."*
6. Continue for several minutes, feeling the smile soften your face and heart.

Smiling physically relaxes your vagus nerve, training your body to associate wealth with warmth instead of worry.

Six Shadow Work Journal Prompts

1. **Joy Wounds:** When did I learn that play or fun was "irresponsible"?
2. **Emotional Programming:** What emotions arise when I imagine being financially secure *and* joyful at the same time?
3. **Permission:** What forms of creativity do I secretly crave but suppress out of fear of wasting time or money?
4. **Embodied Safety:** What physical sensations signal that I feel safe enough to play?
5. **Reclaiming the Artist:** How might my finances improve if I allowed my imagination to lead?
6. **Joy Practice:** What one playful act will I commit to daily or weekly as proof that abundance is safe?

Exercise 3: Play as Ritual

Transform play into a sacred financial ritual. Once a week, do something lighthearted—painting, singing, walking, cooking—and dedicate it as an offering to abundance. Before you begin, say aloud:

"This act of joy honors the child who once felt unsafe to smile. I play now not to escape work, but to invite flow."

In time, your subconscious begins linking money energy with freedom instead of fear, work with delight instead of exhaustion.

The Science of Joyful Earning

Research in neuroeconomics and psychology confirms that positive emotional states increase cognitive flexibility and problem-solving—two core components of successful earning. When you're happy, your prefrontal cortex (responsible for decision-making and planning) works more effectively. You make smarter choices because your brain perceives safety, not threat.

In essence: **joy multiplies competence.** When you approach your career or business with playfulness, you see possibilities others miss. Your creativity becomes currency.

Closing Reflection

Play is not childish—it is sacred rebellion against fear. When you laugh, create, or explore for no reason, you reclaim the freedom that scarcity once stole. Every act of play is a ritual of abundance, a message to your nervous system that the war is over.

You are not here only to survive—you are here to experience the full color of life. And abundance, at its purest form, is not measured in numbers, but in the *ease with which you allow yourself to live.*

Chapter 9: The Architecture of Trust — Rebuilding Your Relationship with Receiving and the Timing of Life

The Heartbeat of Abundance Is Trust

Every financial system—saving, spending, investing, or manifesting—ultimately depends on one thing: **trust.**

Trust that the work you do will yield results.

Trust that when money leaves, it will return.

Trust that the universe, the body, and time itself are not conspiring against you.

But if you grew up amid scarcity or instability, trust was the first thing stolen. You learned early that safety was temporary, promises broke, and comfort vanished without warning. The nervous system adapted by tightening control—gripping, striving, micromanaging every dollar or detail just to feel a hint of certainty.

This chapter is about **rebuilding your internal architecture of trust**—the emotional framework that allows money, opportunity, and timing to flow through your life without constant panic.

Why the Wounded Inner Child Fears Flow

To the inner child, receiving is risky. When you received something as a child—love, a gift, help—it may have come with strings attached or vanished suddenly. Your nervous system learned:

"Receiving isn't safe. It can disappear."

"If I relax, I'll lose everything."

"If I trust, I'll be disappointed."

As an adult, this creates *financial distrust*: the inability to believe that you are supported by life, by timing, or even by your own capability. You might overwork to compensate, hoard to avoid fear, or sabotage new opportunities because they feel too good to be true.

Trust becomes a skill you have to *relearn.*

The Energetics of Trust and Timing

Money operates like water. It moves through systems that are open, clear, and balanced. When fear builds a dam—control, resentment, or self-blame—flow stops. You feel stuck. But the blockage isn't external; it's emotional.

To rebuild trust, you must first understand **timing as intelligence**. Scarcity taught you that delay equals danger. But delay is often a form of preparation. The universe withholds what you're not yet safe to receive.

When your nervous system becomes calm and open, you stop forcing and start aligning. Opportunities begin arriving "on time"—not because life changed, but because *you stopped resisting the rhythm.*

Exercise 1: Mapping the Trust Wound

1. Write down three moments in your life where you felt betrayed or let down—financially or emotionally.
2. Next to each, write what belief about trust was formed (e.g., "People abandon me," "Money disappears," "I can only rely on myself").
3. Look for the common emotional thread—fear of loss, control, or vulnerability.
4. Now, reframe each one into an affirmation of renewed safety. For example:
    - "I can rely on myself *and* allow support."
    - "Money can leave and still return."
    - "I am learning that receiving is safe."

Each rewritten statement begins dismantling the old architecture of fear.

The Nervous System and Receiving Energy

The body's ability to receive is regulated by the *parasympathetic state*—the same system responsible for calm digestion, deep breathing, and connection. When you're in constant fight-or-flight mode, your body interprets *receiving* as vulnerability.

That's why even good news can trigger anxiety—your body doesn't yet believe safety exists in stillness.

Rebuilding this capacity requires practicing **micro-moments of receiving** throughout your day—small experiences that remind your body that trust is safe again.

Exercise 2: The Practice of Small Receiving

1. Each day, notice three moments of gentle receiving:
    - Someone holds a door open for you.
    - You feel warmth from sunlight.
    - You breathe clean air or sip water.
2. When it happens, pause. Breathe. Whisper:
   "I allow this. I am safe to receive."
3. Over time, your nervous system learns that receiving no longer equals loss or obligation.

The more you embody these micro-receivings, the more the macro flows—money, opportunity, generosity—arrive effortlessly.

Visualization: The Bridge of Trust

1. **Close your eyes.** Picture yourself standing on one side of a wide river—the shore of control and fear. On the far side lies abundance, peace, and steady flow.
2. Between you is a shimmering bridge made of light—the Bridge of Trust. Each plank represents a truth you're ready to accept.
3. As you take each step, say:
    - *"I trust my timing."*
    - *"I trust my worth."*
    - *"I trust that what leaves returns multiplied."*
4. When you reach the other side, breathe deeply and feel sunlight on your skin. Whisper:
   "I am safe to live in flow."

This visualization helps the subconscious transition from scarcity-based rigidity to ease-based expansion.

Exercise 3: Trusting Divine Timing

Scarcity trains us to panic when things don't happen fast enough. But divine timing isn't about delay—it's about *alignment.*

1. Think of one financial or life goal that feels "stuck."
2. Ask: *"What might this delay be protecting or preparing me for?"*
3. Write down three ways this time could be serving your healing—perhaps building patience, resilience, or self-trust.
4. Say aloud:
   "I release the need to rush. What is mine will arrive when I am ready to hold it."

This exercise reprograms your nervous system to associate waiting with safety, not danger.

Forging the Pillars of Trust

To rebuild the architecture of trust, imagine it as a temple with five foundational pillars.

1. **Self-Trust** — the belief that you will not abandon yourself in crisis.
    - Practice: speak gently to yourself during financial stress, not critically.
2. **Trust in Flow** — the knowing that what you give and spend circulates back.
    - Practice: bless your money as it leaves—say, *"Return to me in multiplied peace."*
3. **Trust in Timing** — the understanding that slower seasons are gestation, not punishment.
    - Practice: treat waiting as a spiritual inhale, not a void.
4. **Trust in Support** — the willingness to receive help, advice, or collaboration without shame.
    - Practice: allow others to give without apologizing or shrinking.
5. **Trust in Enoughness** — the faith that sufficiency is not a moment, but a mindset.
    - Practice: end each day listing three ways you were "enough" today—financially, emotionally, energetically.

When all five pillars are practiced consistently, your nervous system becomes a structure that can *contain abundance without collapse.*

Meditation: Anchoring into Trust

Purpose: To physically and emotionally stabilize your body in the energy of trust.

1. Sit or lie down comfortably.
2. Inhale through your nose for **four seconds**, imagining golden light entering through the crown of your head.
3. Hold for **two seconds** and whisper, *"I am safe."*
4. Exhale through your mouth for **six seconds**, releasing fear as dark smoke.
5. Place both hands over your heart and repeat slowly:
   "I trust my body. I trust my path. I trust that abundance has not forgotten me."
6. Feel your heartbeat steady and strong—the rhythm of patience and faith.

Practice this daily before checking finances, making big decisions, or entering negotiations. You'll notice the anxiety response softening with repetition.

Six Shadow Work Journal Prompts

1. **Old Lessons:** When was the first time I felt I couldn't trust life to provide?
2. **Control Reflex:** How does fear of uncertainty make me over-control money or outcomes?
3. **Receiving Resistance:** When was the last time I rejected help, praise, or opportunity—and why?
4. **Belief Repair:** What would it mean to fully trust that money can return after leaving?
5. **Emotional Timing:** How does impatience show up in my financial life, and what is it really protecting me from feeling?
6. **Sacred Trust Statement:** Write one sentence that defines what trust means to you now, and read it daily as a vow.

Exercise 4: The Trust Ledger

Create a "Trust Ledger"—a notebook or digital file where you record every instance, big or small, where life *proved itself trustworthy.*

Examples:

- "An unexpected refund arrived."
- "A friend offered help when I needed it."
- "I worried about rent, and it worked out."

Each entry rewires your brain's evidence system. Over time, the ledger becomes proof that life has always been subtly supporting you—even during scarcity.

Closing Reflection

Trust is the final frontier of financial healing. Without it, every dollar feels like sand slipping through your fingers; with it, even small amounts feel infinite.

To trust is to say:

"I no longer confuse control with safety. I can breathe and still be secure."

Rebuilding your architecture of trust does not mean blind optimism—it means grounded faith that you are co-creating with life, not fighting against it. When your nervous system trusts flow, abundance ceases to be a goal and becomes a rhythm.

Chapter 10: Reparenting for Financial Safety

The Full Circle of Healing

You've journeyed through memories, panic, forgiveness, and trust. You've rebuilt safety in your body and learned to see money not as a threat, but as a mirror. Now, it's time to bring all those lessons home—to the *relationship between your adult self and your inner child.*

Reparenting is the process of becoming the caregiver you never had. It means meeting your own needs for security, consistency, and love—especially where those needs were unmet around money.

When you reparent yourself financially, you rewrite the most powerful message your body ever learned:

"No one is coming to save me."

Through conscious care, you now teach your inner child:

"Someone is here—you."

What Financial Reparenting Really Means

Reparenting is not about perfection. It's about *presence.* You don't have to make every "right" choice. You only need to stay connected when fear or guilt appear.

Financial reparenting looks like this:

- When fear arises, you *listen* instead of suppress.
- When panic returns, you *soothe* instead of scold.
- When scarcity tempts self-blame, you *respond* with reassurance: *"I know why you're scared, but I've got us now."*

In that simple exchange, the past begins to dissolve. The child learns safety through your consistent care, and the adult learns power through compassion.

The Three Core Roles of the Financial Parent

1. The Protector

The protector sets emotional and financial boundaries. They handle bills, deadlines, and decisions. They create structure without punishment.

When your protector is active, your inner child can rest. You no longer need to hustle for safety—it's built into your system.

Say aloud:

"I protect us through clarity, not fear. I manage money as an act of love."

2. The Provider

The provider ensures nourishment—not only physical needs like food or shelter, but also emotional nourishment like rest, joy, and creative play.

Ask yourself:

"What does my inner child need this week to feel cared for?"

Sometimes it's saving extra money; sometimes it's a soft blanket, a warm bath, or one afternoon without obligations. The provider reminds your inner child that abundance includes *comfort*, not just survival.

3. The Nurturer

The nurturer speaks the language of compassion. When shame arises, this voice answers gently:

"You are learning."

"You don't have to be perfect."

"We are safe even when things change."

The nurturer is how love rewires the nervous system. It replaces the inner critic with the tone of healing.

Exercise 1: Writing the Financial Parenting Contract

1. On paper, write: *"I, [your name], agree to care for my inner child financially, emotionally, and energetically."*
2. Below it, list your promises:
    - "I will check our finances with calm, not panic."
    - "I will plan for joy, not just emergencies."
    - "I will not shame us for learning slowly."
    - "I will never leave us in confusion without comfort."
3. Sign and date it.
4. Place it somewhere visible—a reminder that healing is now under your supervision.

Every time fear arises, revisit this contract. It's your sacred agreement of consistency, the very thing you always needed from others.

Healing the Parent-Child Split Around Money

When you face financial stress, two selves emerge:

- The *inner child*, who remembers instability and shame.
- The *inner parent*, who wants control and certainty.

Most people let these parts argue—one begging for freedom, the other enforcing restriction. Reparenting means **uniting them** instead of letting them battle.

Try this exercise:

1. Sit quietly. Place one hand on your heart and the other on your stomach.
2. Imagine your heart as the *adult self*—grounded, calm, compassionate.
3. Imagine your stomach as the *inner child*—sensitive, reactive, honest.
4. Let them have a conversation:
    - Adult: *"I know money feels scary."*
    - Child: *"I just don't want us to lose everything again."*
    - Adult: *"We won't. I have a plan, and you can rest."*

Feel the energy between your hands soften as unity replaces conflict.

Exercise 2: Creating the Financial Safety Routine

Reparenting thrives in repetition. Your nervous system learns safety through *predictability.*

Create a weekly ritual that reinforces security:

1. The Check-In (5 minutes)

Ask yourself: "What's one financial win this week, no matter how small?" Celebrate it.

2. The Review (10 minutes)

Look over your budget gently, as you would a child's report card—with encouragement, not criticism.

3. The Nurture Moment (10 minutes)

Do something soothing afterward: listen to music, light a candle, or drink tea.

This signals your body that money management can coexist with relaxation.

Visualization: The Home of Safety

1. Close your eyes. Imagine a cozy home built by your adult self—solid walls, gentle light, warmth in every room.
2. Inside sits your inner child, perhaps still anxious.
3. Walk over and kneel beside them. Say:
   "This home will never disappear. You belong here. We are safe now."
4. Hand them a small key made of golden light and say:
   "This is the key to our safety. You can always come here."
5. As the child takes it, the walls glow brighter, symbolizing stability.

This visualization helps the subconscious anchor safety as a *felt experience,* not just an idea.

Meditation: The Adult Voice of Calm

Purpose: To strengthen the new internal authority that replaces fear with compassion.

1. Sit comfortably. Inhale through your nose for **four seconds**, exhale through your mouth for **six**.
2. Say softly:
   "I am the adult now. I am capable. I am kind."
3. Visualize your younger self standing in front of you.
4. With each breath, imagine wrapping them in a warm light that expands from your chest.
5. Whisper:
   "You never have to worry about money alone again. I'm here now."
6. Stay until you feel warmth or tears—both are signs that connection has formed.

Repeat this meditation before major financial decisions or when anxiety flares.

Exercise 3: The Reparented Money Plan

Now that your adult self and inner child are allies, design your money plan together.

Divide a page into two columns:

- **Adult Perspective:** Logic, strategy, goals, timelines.
- **Inner Child Perspective:** Feelings, needs, comfort, play.

For each financial decision—saving, investing, buying—ask both sides:

- "Does this make us feel safe?"
- "Does this make us feel cared for?"

For example:

- Adult: "We'll save $200 this month."
- Child: "Can we also keep $20 for something fun?"
- Adult: "Yes, because joy *is* part of safety."

By blending structure and softness, your money system becomes emotionally sustainable.

Exercise 4: Inner Child Journaling Dialogue

Set a timer for 10 minutes. Write a conversation between "You (Adult)" and "Little Me." Use different handwriting or colors if possible.

Example:

Little Me: "I'm scared to look at our bank account."

You: "I know. It used to mean bad news. But now it's just numbers telling our story."

Little Me: "Will it ever stop being scary?"

You: "Yes, when we check it together with love instead of fear."

Read the conversation aloud. Each time you do, the old terror loses its hold.

Six Shadow Work Journal Prompts

1. **Parental Echoes:** What phrases about money did my caregivers use that still echo in my mind?
2. **Emotional Substitution:** How did my family use money to show—or withhold—love?
3. **Caretaking Reversal:** When did I first feel responsible for my family's financial emotions?
4. **Reparenting Blueprint:** What words and actions now define me as my own caregiver?
5. **Safety Reframed:** How can I remind myself that structure and consistency equal love, not control?
6. **Integration:** What does my inner child most need to hear before each financial decision?

Exercise 5: Building the Reparented Altar

Create a small altar or sacred space that represents financial safety. Include:

- A candle for clarity.
- A coin or bill to symbolize flow.
- A photo or drawing representing your younger self.
- A small note that reads, *"I provide safety now."*

Light the candle during budgeting, journaling, or meditation sessions. Over time, this ritual embeds the feeling of protection into your financial routine.

Signs You're Successfully Reparenting

- You check finances without immediate panic.
- You allow joy or rest without guilt.
- You can comfort yourself during uncertainty instead of spiraling.
- You make choices from stability, not reaction.
- You no longer abandon yourself when scared—you turn inward and say, *"I'm here."*

When these become consistent, your financial healing is not theory—it's embodied truth.

Closing Reflection: The Guardian of Stability

You began this journey as someone haunted by financial fear. Now, you stand as your own guardian—a protector, provider, and nurturer unified in strength.

Reparenting is not the end of healing; it's the beginning of mastery. It's the daily act of proving to your inner child that love can be consistent, that safety can be sustained, and that abundance is not something to chase, but something you *become.*

Each time you speak kindly to yourself, each time you pause instead of panic, each time you check your balance with compassion—you are repairing an ancient fracture.

You are no longer the frightened child waiting for rescue.
You are the adult who came back for them.

And that, above all else, is financial safety.

Appendix A: Inner Child Letter Prompts

Introduction: Writing as Healing Dialogue

Writing to your inner child is one of the most powerful ways to transform unprocessed emotion into safety.
It bridges time, turning fragmented memories into conversation—and conversation into connection.

Letters allow you to communicate across the emotional timeline: your present, capable self reaching back to comfort the child who still lives inside you. In this appendix, you will find structured **Inner Child Letter Prompts** designed specifically to heal financial trauma, scarcity conditioning, guilt, and trust wounds.

Each letter is an invitation to deepen your reparenting practice. These prompts are not for performance or perfection—they are for intimacy. Your words are medicine.

Take your time. Write slowly, honestly, and by hand if possible. Feel your breathing as you write. Let each sentence carry warmth, not analysis.

Before you begin, you may want to create a simple ritual space:

- Light a candle or place your hand over your heart.
- Whisper: *"I am safe to remember, safe to release, safe to heal."*
- Begin writing when you feel grounded.

Section 1: Letters of Acknowledgment

For seeing what was once unseen.

These prompts help you name experiences your younger self could not articulate. The goal is recognition—bringing forgotten pain into the light without judgment.

1. **The First Scarcity Memory:**
    - "Dear Little Me, I remember the first time you felt there wasn't enough..."
    - Describe the scene in detail: sounds, smells, sensations. Then, write what you wish someone had told you in that moment.
2. **The Moment You Learned to Fear Money:**
    - "Dear Little Me, you didn't deserve to carry that fear..."
    - Describe who modeled anxiety or scarcity around money. How did it make you feel about safety, love, or self-worth?
3. **The Unheard Child:**
    - "Dear Little Me, no one listened when you said you were scared..."
    - Write the words your child-self wanted to say but couldn't. Then, respond to those words as your adult self—with empathy and assurance.
4. **The Forgotten Joy:**
    - "Dear Little Me, I remember when you laughed freely..."
    - Recall a joyful moment from childhood, especially one unrelated to material wealth. Let it remind you that joy and safety can coexist.
5. **The Abandoned Dream:**
    - "Dear Little Me, you once wanted to be..."
    - Revisit a dream that money fears or external pressures made you abandon. Tell your younger self it's not too late to play again.

Section 2: Letters of Compassion

For replacing shame with understanding.

Compassion letters teach your nervous system that love can coexist with mistakes, and that financial missteps are not moral failures.

1. **The Letter of Forgiveness:**
    - "Dear Me, I forgive you for every time you acted from fear."
    - Describe specific moments—overspending, avoidance, guilt—and explain the emotional context behind them. Validate your humanity.
2. **The Letter of Survival:**
    - "Dear Me, you did what you had to do."
    - Acknowledge how survival instincts shaped your choices. Replace criticism with gratitude: *"You kept us alive."*
3. **The Letter to the One Who Tried Too Hard:**
    - "Dear Me, I see how hard you've worked to earn safety."
    - Speak to the overachiever in you who equated worth with productivity. Offer them rest.
4. **The Letter of Release:**
    - "Dear Me, I release the belief that I must struggle to deserve."
    - Write each limiting belief on separate lines, then symbolically "cross it out" with loving statements of truth.
5. **The Letter of Enoughness:**
    - "Dear Me, you are enough even when you rest."
    - Describe what it feels like to imagine financial peace without fear. Allow yourself to picture safety that doesn't require exhaustion.

Section 3: Letters of Reassurance

For calming the nervous system and creating emotional regulation.

These letters anchor the adult voice as the new caregiver—predictable, consistent, and kind.

1. **The Safety Letter:**
    - "Dear Little Me, I will never let you go hungry, unseen, or unheard again."
    - Describe the systems and habits you've built to ensure safety (budgeting, grounding, emotional awareness).
2. **The Security Letter:**
    - "Dear Little Me, it's safe to exhale now."
    - Remind your child-self that financial chaos no longer controls your life. Offer tangible proof of stability in the present.
3. **The Consistency Letter:**
    - "Dear Little Me, I will show up every week."
    - Write a promise to maintain weekly check-ins, gentle financial reviews, or self-soothing rituals. The tone should feel steady and calm.
4. **The Comfort Letter:**
    - "Dear Little Me, you deserve warmth and ease."
    - Name sensory comforts—blankets, baths, nature walks—that make your inner child feel secure.
5. **The Reassurance Letter:**
    - "Dear Me, no matter what happens, I'll handle it with love."
    - Describe how you'll talk to yourself during future stress. Write out the exact words you'll use when fear returns.

Section 4: Letters of Reconnection
For building emotional intimacy and rediscovering trust.

1. **The Letter to the Wounded Child:**
    - "Dear Little Me, I see the pain you carried that wasn't yours."
    - Name the burdens you took on from adults—debt, emotional caretaking, guilt—and return them symbolically to the universe.
2. **The Letter to the Parent Within:**
    - "Dear Inner Parent, thank you for learning how to care for us."
    - Acknowledge your adult self's evolution. Celebrate the progress you've made in regulating your emotions and finances.
3. **The Letter to Money Itself:**
    - "Dear Money, I'm ready for a new relationship."
    - Treat money as a living entity. Write about how fear damaged the relationship and what safety looks like now.
4. **The Letter to Trust:**
    - "Dear Trust, I'm learning to let you back in."
    - Reflect on how timing, patience, and faith are becoming easier to hold.
5. **The Letter to the Future Self:**
    - "Dear Future Me, thank you for building the life we once feared was impossible."
    - Describe your future daily life of safety, abundance, and calm as if it already exists.

Section 5: Letters of Integration

For blending the healed self with the present moment.

These letters bring closure to the healing arc, allowing your inner child and adult self to merge into partnership.

1. **The Letter of Gratitude:**
    - "Dear Little Me, thank you for surviving so I could thrive."
    - Express appreciation for your inner child's endurance. Gratitude finalizes the healing cycle.
2. **The Letter of Merging:**
    - "Dear Me, we are one now."
    - Write as if the line between your child-self and adult self dissolves. Describe what it feels like to live as a unified being.
3. **The Letter of Celebration:**
    - "Dear Me, I am proud of you."
    - Name specific emotional victories—checking your finances calmly, saying no without fear, or feeling safe in ease.
4. **The Letter of Continuance:**
    - "Dear Me, our healing will keep unfolding."
    - Write about the next step in your growth. Reaffirm that healing is a lifelong conversation, not a finish line.
5. **The Letter of Legacy:**
    - "Dear Me, I will pass on what I've learned."
    - Imagine teaching others—your children, friends, or community—the compassion and wisdom you've gained. This final letter grounds your healing in service.

Writing Tips for Emotional Safety

- **Set a time limit:** 15–20 minutes per session helps avoid overwhelm.
- **Pause when triggered:** If tears or tension rise, place your hand over your heart and breathe until calm. Resume only when ready.
- **End every letter with a soothing statement:** *"We are safe now."* or *"I love you exactly as you are."*
- **Ritualize completion:** Burn or fold the letter respectfully. You may keep some in a journal dedicated to your inner child.

Closing Reflection: Letters as Lifelines

Every letter is a bridge—between fear and safety, past and present, scarcity and sufficiency.

Your handwriting becomes the proof of reunion, the voice your younger self waited decades to hear.

When you write, you are no longer revisiting pain; you are rescuing the one who felt abandoned inside it. Each word is a promise:

"You were never the problem. You were the one who deserved care all along."

Return to these prompts anytime you feel disconnected, afraid, or unworthy. The child within you will always listen—and now, they'll always be answered.

Appendix B: Visualization Ritual for Safety & Trust

Introduction: Why Visualization Heals Financial Trauma

When you've lived in prolonged scarcity or emotional neglect, the body no longer differentiates between *memory* and *imagination.*
The same physiological responses—tension, heart rate changes, adrenaline—can be triggered by a thought as easily as by a real event.
This is both the problem *and* the cure.

Visualization rituals use the body's own sensory intelligence to rewrite those old emotional associations. By reimagining safety, you *teach your nervous system what safety feels like.*
When practiced regularly, these visualizations reshape neural pathways, gently replacing fear with calm, uncertainty with trust, and scarcity with the embodied experience of "enough."

The following three rituals are designed to be immersive, vivid, and deeply grounding.
Each one activates the **parasympathetic nervous system**—the body's natural safety mode—while strengthening your emotional relationship with abundance, stability, and flow.

You may wish to:

- Practice them in a quiet space with dim light.
- Use a soft instrumental background track or ambient sounds.
- Sit or lie comfortably, one hand over your heart and one over your abdomen.
- End each ritual by journaling or speaking aloud one sentence that anchors what you experienced.

Ritual 1: The Inner Vault of Safety

(For grounding, protection, and stability.)

This ritual is designed to help you establish a felt sense of financial and emotional security—a sacred "inner vault" that holds your energy, worth, and resources.

It trains the nervous system to perceive *safety as permanent,* not temporary.

Preparation

Light a candle or hold an object that symbolizes security to you (a coin, a stone, or even your hand over your heart).

Take three deep breaths.

Inhale through your nose for **four seconds**, exhale through your mouth for **six.**

As you breathe, imagine your breath forming an invisible protective circle around your body.

Visualization

1. **Enter the Vault:**
   Close your eyes and imagine walking through a hallway carved from soft, glowing stone.
   The air is warm and golden, humming with calm. At the end of the hall, a large circular door waits—engraved with symbols of protection.
2. **Unlocking:**
   In your hand, you hold a key shaped like your heartbeat.
   With one slow inhale, insert the key into the vault door.
   With your exhale, the lock clicks open—not from force, but from recognition.

3.Inside the Vault:

Step inside. The vault glows from within. Shelves line the walls, each holding something that represents safety in your life: your resilience, your compassion, your ability to rebuild.

The floor beneath you pulses gently, matching your breath.

4.

Sealing Safety:

Walk to the center of the vault and kneel. Place your palms on the ground.

Feel warmth rising from the floor into your chest.

Say aloud or in your mind:

"I am safe in my body. I am safe with money. I am safe in this world."

5.Closing the Door with Trust:

As you leave the vault, the door remains open—not to expose you, but to remind you that safety doesn't need to be locked away anymore.

The vault exists within you always, accessible by breath.

Integration

When finished, open your eyes and place both hands over your heart. Repeat slowly:

"Safety lives in me now."

You may draw or write what your vault looked like.

Revisit this visualization before financial tasks or after stressful interactions—it anchors your body back to protection and self-trust.

Ritual 2: The River of Trust

(For restoring flow, surrender, and belief in timing.)

Trust requires movement. Scarcity freezes energy; trust lets it flow again.

This ritual reawakens your inner rhythm with life's timing—the sense that you can release control and still be carried.

Preparation

Dim the lights or face a window with soft natural light.

Visualize a slow current of breath through your body—inhale rising from your feet to your chest, exhale descending from your chest to your feet.

This prepares the body to enter flow-state.

Visualization

1. **The Approach:**
   Picture yourself standing at the edge of a wide, crystal-blue river.
   The water sparkles under a soft sun. The current moves steadily—neither rushing nor stagnant.
   This is the **River of Trust.** It represents the natural flow of life and resources.
2. **Stepping In:**
   Dip one foot into the water.
   The temperature is perfect—cool enough to awaken, warm enough to comfort.
   Whisper:

"I am safe to be carried."

As you wade deeper, the water rises to your knees, your waist, your chest. Each inch dissolves a layer of control, fear, or rigidity.

4.Surrendering to Flow:

When you feel ready, lean back and float.

The river supports you completely.

You can breathe easily; the water feels like silk around your body.

It whispers words of reassurance:

"You are not late. You are not forgotten. You are always held."

5.Trust in Timing:

Look up and see the sky slowly shifting through colors—gold, rose, blue, indigo.

These represent the cycles of life: earning, spending, saving, resting.

Notice how the river carries you effortlessly through each one.

6.Receiving:

Downstream, the current delivers small gifts to your hands—a coin, a feather, a leaf, a spark of light.

These symbolize unexpected blessings and opportunities that flow naturally when you are open.

Hold them to your heart and whisper:

"What is meant for me will always find me."

Integration

Step gently out of the river, glowing and renewed.

Dry yourself in golden sunlight. Feel your feet on solid earth again, but notice—the ground no longer feels heavy. It feels supportive.

Journal the experience, finishing with this affirmation:

"I am aligned with life's timing. I trust what flows and what stays."

Practice this ritual anytime you feel panic about delays, missed chances, or scarcity. It restores patience, receptivity, and ease.

Ritual 3: The Circle of Receiving

(For building openness, worthiness, and the ability to accept abundance.)

The ability to receive is often the final step in healing financial trauma.
When early neglect taught you that love and support were conditional, your body learned to equate receiving with danger.
This visualization retrains your system to experience *receiving as nourishment.*

Preparation

Sit or lie comfortably.
Hold your palms open, facing upward on your lap or by your sides.
Lightly close your eyes and breathe deeply, feeling the air fill your chest like sunlight filling a room.

Visualization

1. **The Circle Forms:**
   Picture yourself standing in the center of a glowing circle of light.
   Around you stand many luminous figures—your healed selves, ancestors, mentors, or spiritual guides.
   Each one holds a lantern representing wisdom, kindness, and generosity.
2. **The Invitation:**
   One by one, they approach you and offer their light.
   Some hand you a lantern, others simply place a hand over your heart.
   Each time, breathe in deeply and whisper:

"I receive this with gratitude and safety."

Feel the warmth collecting inside you, layer upon layer, until your chest glows like a sunrise.

3.Rewriting the Body's Response:

Notice any resistance—tightness in the stomach, a lump in the throat.
Instead of pushing it away, breathe gently into it.
Say:

"It's safe to receive. Nothing bad happens when I am cared for."

With each exhale, imagine the resistance melting into golden light.

4.Expanding the Circle:

Now, your own light begins to glow brighter.
The circle expands outward—your radiance touches every being, every home, every space.
The energy you receive doesn't hoard; it multiplies and circulates.
Whisper:

"As I receive, I naturally give. Abundance moves through me with love."

5.The Integration of Worth:

Step into the center of your light and see your inner child standing there.
Kneel before them and hold out your glowing hands.
Say:

"You never have to earn love or support again. You were born deserving."

Hand them one of the lanterns. Watch as they smile, radiant and calm.

Integration

When you open your eyes, stay seated for a moment with palms still facing up.

Let your breath slow and whisper softly:

"I am safe to receive. I am safe to shine. I am safe to trust life's generosity."

Journal any sensations or emotions that surfaced. Over time, you'll notice that compliments, help, and money feel easier to accept—without guilt or fear.

Closing Reflection: Returning to the Body as Home

Safety and trust do not live outside you—they live *within your nervous system.*

Every visualization you perform strengthens the pathways of stability, turning survival energy into creative energy.

Each ritual tells your body:

"We are no longer waiting for safety. We are creating it."

Practice these visualizations regularly—especially before major financial decisions, during moments of anxiety, or at the start of your day. With each session, you'll notice your breathing deepen, your shoulders lower, your thoughts slow.

That is the sensation of healing taking root—

safety restored, trust remembered, abundance reclaimed.

Appendix C: Shadow Work Prompts for Inner Financial Healing — 50 Transformational Questions

Introduction: Meeting the Financial Shadow

Shadow work is the process of revealing the parts of yourself that were hidden, suppressed, or shamed—often because they were once unsafe to express.

When it comes to money, your **shadow** holds the memories of fear, guilt, greed, unworthiness, and resentment that quietly influence every decision you make.

You may not consciously think, "I'm afraid to be wealthy," but your nervous system might still associate abundance with abandonment, judgment, or loss. The financial shadow isn't evil—it's *misunderstood.* By bringing light to it, you no longer have to be ruled by unconscious emotional programs.

The following **50 transformational questions** are designed to help you explore, release, and reprogram those hidden stories. Each prompt is divided into thematic sections that reflect the stages of emotional recovery outlined throughout this book—from fear and scarcity to trust, receiving, and self-leadership.

Use them as meditative reflections, journaling exercises, or even as part of spoken self-dialogue. There are no right or wrong answers—only truth seeking to be known.

Before beginning, take a slow breath and affirm:

"I am safe to see what has been unseen. I explore not to judge, but to understand."

Section 1: Confronting the Scarcity Wound (1–10)
Understanding where fear of lack first began.

1. What is my earliest memory of not having enough—whether money, affection, or safety?
2. How did my caregivers react to financial stress, and what did I learn by watching them?
3. What emotions—fear, anger, shame—do I associate most strongly with the word "money"?
4. In what ways did scarcity become part of my identity or family culture?
5. What physical sensations arise in my body when I think about spending or losing money?
6. Did I ever witness love being withdrawn or given based on money?
7. What messages did I absorb about "rich people," and how do they influence me today?
8. How does my nervous system respond to financial uncertainty—freeze, overwork, or avoid?
9. What part of me still believes that struggle equals worth?
10. How do I unconsciously recreate the chaos or scarcity of my childhood in adulthood?

Section 2: Healing Guilt and Shame Around Money (11–20)
Releasing emotional debt that blocks abundance.

1. What financial mistakes do I still hold against myself, even after years have passed?
2. Who taught me to feel ashamed about needing or wanting help?
3. What do I believe would happen if I became financially secure and others didn't?
4. When did I first learn that pleasure or luxury was "selfish"?
5. In what situations do I punish myself for having money, through overspending or neglect?
6. Do I secretly believe that good people must stay modest, poor, or struggling to prove virtue?
7. How does guilt appear when I try to rest or enjoy what I've earned?
8. Who benefits emotionally from my financial guilt—me, my family, or old beliefs?
9. What would it mean to fully forgive myself for every past money decision?
10. How would my life change if I stopped apologizing for wanting more?

Section 3: The Control–Fear Loop (21–30)
Recognizing the behaviors that mimic safety but limit flow.

1. Where do I micromanage money to avoid feeling out of control?
2. How does overworking or "doing more" become a coping mechanism for anxiety?
3. What am I afraid might happen if I stopped checking, planning, or worrying constantly?
4. What areas of life do I try to control because I don't trust the universe or myself?
5. What specific event convinced me that I must handle everything alone?
6. How does perfectionism appear in my financial decisions?
7. What would surrender look like if I trusted life's timing?
8. What emotions arise when I imagine delegating or asking for help?
9. Do I equate relaxation with danger or laziness? Why?
10. How can I practice releasing control daily without feeling unsafe?

Section 4: Reclaiming the Right to Receive (31–40)

Expanding your nervous system's capacity for abundance and support.

1. When was the last time I struggled to accept help, a compliment, or generosity?
2. What fears arise when I imagine receiving large amounts of money or recognition?
3. Whose voice inside me says, "You don't deserve that much"?
4. What was modeled for me about receiving—was it celebrated or shamed?
5. How do I react physically when someone gives to me freely?
6. What would it feel like to receive without earning, proving, or performing?
7. How do I sabotage opportunities because they feel "too easy"?
8. What sensations in my body signal openness vs. resistance to receiving?
9. What practices help me associate receiving with safety rather than danger?
10. How can I show gratitude without guilt when life supports me unexpectedly?

Section 5: Trust, Timing, and Surrender (41–45)
Transforming anxiety about the unknown into faith in process.

1. Where in my life do I feel impatient with progress, and what fear hides beneath that impatience?
2. How have past disappointments affected my willingness to trust timing?
3. What evidence do I already have that life or the universe has supported me?
4. How would my daily life change if I truly believed that what's meant for me will arrive?
5. When do I confuse waiting with failure, and how can I redefine waiting as growth?

Section 6: Empowered Stewardship and Self-Trust (46–50)
Integrating healing into leadership, confidence, and autonomy.

1. In what ways do I still doubt my ability to manage money wisely?
2. How can I practice being a calm leader of my finances, rather than a fearful manager?
3. What does self-trust feel like in my body, and how can I cultivate it daily?
4. How can I use money as a tool for stability, creativity, and service rather than validation?
5. What vow do I want to make today to the child within me who once felt unsafe about money?

How to Work With These Prompts

1. **Choose intuitively.**
   Don't move through them mechanically. Each question holds emotional weight. Let your intuition select the ones that resonate most on a given day.
2. **Respond with sensory awareness.**
   As you write, notice how your body reacts—tightness, warmth, tears, sighs. These sensations are your nervous system releasing energy.
3. **Pause for compassion.**
   If you encounter resistance or discomfort, place your hand on your heart and whisper, *"It's okay to feel this."* You're not reliving trauma—you're reclaiming control.
4. **Revisit periodically.**
   The same prompt may yield deeper truths over time. Healing is cyclical, not linear.
5. **End each session with grounding.**
   After writing, take three slow breaths. Stretch, sip water, or perform the "Vault of Safety" visualization from Appendix B to close the energetic container.

Closing Reflection: Integrating the Shadow Into Light

The financial shadow isn't an enemy—it's an archive. Within it lives every strategy you ever used to survive scarcity, neglect, and fear. Shadow work doesn't erase those patterns—it **transforms** them.

As you move through these 50 prompts, remember:

- Every answer is a door back to your power.
- Every insight brings you closer to trust.
- Every acknowledgment releases the tension that once kept you in survival mode.

Your goal is not to become fearless—it's to become *present.* When you can face your fears with compassion, you end the war between your inner child and your adult self.

And in that peace, abundance begins to flow—not because you've forced it, but because you've finally created space for it to arrive.

Message from the Author:

I hope you enjoyed this book, I love astrology and knew there was not a book such as this out on the shelf. I love metaphysical items as well. Please check out my other books:

-Life of Government Benefits

-My life of Hell

-My life with Hydrocephalus

-Red Sky

-World Domination:Woman's rule

-World Domination:Woman's Rule 2: The War

-Life and Banishment of Apophis: book 1

-The Kidney Friendly Diet

-The Ultimate Hemp Cookbook

-Creating a Dispensary(legally)

-Cleanliness throughout life: the importance of showering from childhood to adulthood.

-Strong Roots: The Risks of Overcoddling children

-Hemp Horoscopes: Cosmic Insights and Earthly Healing

- Celestial Hemp Navigating the Zodiac: Through the Green Cosmos

-Astrological Hemp: Aligning The Stars with Earth's Ancient Herb

-The Astrological Guide to Hemp: Stars, Signs, and Sacred Leaves

-Green Growth: Innovative Marketing Strategies for your Hemp Products and Dispensary

-Cosmic Cannabis

-Astrological Munchies

-Henry The Hemp

-Zodiacal Roots: The Astrological Soul Of Hemp

- **Green Constellations: Intersection of Hemp and Zodiac**

-Hemp in The Houses: An astrological Adventure Through The Cannabis Galaxy

-Galactic Ganja Guide
Heavenly Hemp
Zodiac Leaves
Doctor Who Astrology
Cannastrology
Stellar Satvias and Cosmic Indicas
Celestial Cannabis: A Zodiac Journey
AstroHerbology: The Sky and The Soil: Volume 1
AstroHerbology:Celestial Cannabis:Volume 2
Cosmic Cannabis Cultivation
The Starry Guide to Herbal Harmony: Volume 1
The Starry Guide to Herbal Harmony: Cannabis Universe: Volume 2
Yugioh Astrology: Astrological Guide to Deck, Duels and more
Nightmare Mansion: Echoes of The Abyss
Nightmare Mansion 2: Legacy of Shadows
Nightmare Mansion 3: Shadows of the Forgotten
Nightmare Mansion 4: Echoes of the Damned
The Life and Banishment of Apophis: Book 2
Nightmare Mansion: Halls of Despair
Healing with Herb: Cannabis and Hydrocephalus
Planetary Pot: Aligning with Astrological Herbs: Volume 1
Fast Track to Freedom: 30 Days to Financial Independence Using AI, Assets, and Agile Hustles
Cosmic Hemp Pathways
How to Become Financially Free in 30 Days: 10,000 Paths to Prosperity
Zodiacal Herbage: Astrological Insights: Volume 1
Nightmare Mansion: Whispers in the Walls
The Daleks Invade Atlantis
Henry the hemp and Hydrocephalus

10X The Kidney Friendly Diet

Cannabis Universe: Adult coloring book

Hemp Astrology: The Healing Power of the Stars

Zodiacal Herbage: Astrological Insights: Cannabis Universe: Volume 2

Planetary Pot: Aligning with Astrological Herbs: Cannabis Universes: Volume 2

Doctor Who: Convergence Protocol – The Replicator War

Nightmare Mansion: Curse of the Blood Moon

The Celestial Stoner: A Guide to the Zodiac

Cosmic Pleasures: Sex Toy Astrology for Every Sign

Hydrocephalus Astrology: Navigating the Stars and Healing Waters

Lapis and the Mischievous Chocolate Bar

Celestial Positions: Sexual Astrology for Every Sign

Apophis's Shadow Work Journal: **:** A Journey of Self-Discovery and Healing

Kinky Cosmos: Sexual Kink Astrology for Every Sign

Digital Cosmos: The Astrological Digimon Compendium

Stellar Seeds: The Cosmic Guide to Growing with Astrology

Apophis's Daily Gratitude Journal

Cat Astrology: Feline Mysteries of the Cosmos

The Cosmic Kama Sutra: An Astrological Guide to Sexual Positions

Unleash Your Potential: A Guided Journal Powered by AI Insights

Whispers of the Enchanted Grove

Cosmic Pleasures: An Astrological Guide to Sexual Kinks

369, 12 Manifestation Journal

Whisper of the nocturne journal(blank journal for writing or drawing)

The Boogey Book

Locked In Reflection: A Chastity Journey Through Locktober

Generating Wealth Quickly:How to Generate $100,000 in 24 Hours

Star Magic: Harness the Power of the Universe

The Flatulence Chronicles: A Fart Journal for Self-Discovery

The Doctor and The Death Moth

Seize the Day: A Personal Seizure Tracking Journal

The Ultimate Boogeyman Safari: A Journey into the Boogie World and Beyond

Whispers of Samhain: 1,000 Spells of Love, Luck, and Lunar Magic: Samhain Spell Book

Apophis's guides:Witch's Spellbook Crafting Guide for Halloween

Frost & Flame: The Enchanted Yule Grimoire of 1000 Winter Spells

The Ultimate Boogey Goo Guide & Spooky Activities for Halloween Fun

Harmony of the Scales: A Libra's Spellcraft for Balance and Beauty

The Enchanted Advent: 36 Days of Christmas Wonders

Nightmare Mansion: The Labyrinth of Screams

Harvest of Enchantment: 1,000 Spells of Gratitude, Love, and Fortune for Thanksgiving

The Boogey Chronicles: A Journal of Nightly Encounters and Shadowy Secrets

The 12 Days of Financial Freedom: A Step-by-Step Christmas Countdown to Transform Your Finances

Sigil of the Eternal Spiral Blank Journal

A Christmas Feast: Timeless Recipes for Every Meal

Holiday Stress-Free Solutions: A Survival Guide to Thriving During the Festive Season

Yu-Gi-Oh! Holiday Gifting Mastery: The Ultimate Guide for Fans and Newcomers Alike

Holiday Harmony: A Hydrocephalus Survival Guide for the Festive Season

Celestial Craft: The Witch's Almanac for 2025 – A Cosmic Guide to Manifestations, Moons, and Mystical Events

Doctor Who: The Toymaker's Winter Wonderland

Tulsa King Unveiled: A Thrilling Guide to Stallone's Mafia Masterpiece

Pendulum Craft: A Complete Guide to Crafting and Using Personalized Divination Tools

Nightmare Mansion: Santa's Eternal Eve

Starlight Noel: A Cosmic Journey through Christmas Mysteries

The Dark Architect: Unlocking the Blueprint of Existence

Surviving the Embrace: The Ultimate Guide to Encounters with The Hugging Molly

The Enchanted Codex: Secrets of the Craft for Witches, Wiccans, and Pagans

Harvest of Gratitude: A Complete Thanksgiving Guide

Yuletide Essentials: A Complete Guide to an Authentic and Magical Christmas

Celestial Smokes: A Cosmic Guide to Cigars and Astrology

Living in Balance: A Comprehensive Survival Guide to Thriving with Diabetes Insipidus

Cosmic Symbiosis: The Venom Zodiac Chronicles

The Cursed Paw of Ambition

Cosmic Symbiosis: The Astrological Venom Journal

Celestial Wonders Unfold: A Stargazer's Guide to the Cosmos (2024-2029)

The Ultimate Black Friday Prepper's Guide: Mastering Shopping Strategies and Savings

Cosmic Sales: The Astrological Guide to Black Friday Shopping

Legends of the Corn Mother and Other Harvest Myths

Whispers of the Harvest: The Corn Mother's Journal

The Evergreen Spellbook

The Doctor Meets the Boogeyman

The White Witch of Rose Hall's SpellBook

The Gingerbread Golem's Shadow: A Study in Sweet Darkness

The Gingerbread Golem Codex: An Academic Exploration of Sweet Myths

The Gingerbread Golem Grimoire: Sweet Magicks and Spells for the Festive Witch

The Curse of the Gingerbread Golem

10-minute Christmas Crafts for kids

Christmas Crisis Solutions: The Ultimate Last-Minute Survival Guide

Gingerbread Golem Recipes: Holiday Treats with a Magical Twist

The Infinite Key: Unlocking Mystical Secrets of the Ages

Enchanted Yule: A Wiccan and Pagan Guide to a Magical and Memorable Season

Dinosaurs of Power: Unlocking Ancient Magick

Astro-Dinos: The Cosmic Guide to Prehistoric Wisdom

Gallifrey's Yule Logs: A Festive Doctor Who Cookbook

The Dino Grimoire: Secrets of Prehistoric Magick

The Gift They Never Knew They Needed

The Gingerbread Golem's Culinary Alchemy: Enchanting Recipes for a Sweetly Dark Feast

A Time Lord Christmas: Holiday Adventures with the Doctor

Krampusproofing Your Home: Defensive Strategies for Yule

Silent Frights: A Collection of Christmas Creepypastas to Chill Your Bones

Santa Raptor's Jolly Carnage: A Dino-Claus Christmas Tale

Prehistoric Palettes: A Dino Wicca Coloring Journey

The Christmas Wishkeeper Chronicles

The Starlight Sleigh: A Holiday Journey

Elf Secrets: The True Magic of the North Pole

Candy Cane Conjurations

Cooking with Kids: Recipes Under 20 Minutes

Doctor Who: The TARDIS Confiscation

The Anxiety First Aid Kit: Quick Tools to Calm Your Mind

Frosty Whispers: A Winter's Tale

The Infinite Key: Unlocking the Secrets to Prosperity, Resilience, and Purpose

The Grasping Void: Why You'll Regret This Purchase

Astrology for Busy Bees: Star Signs Simplified

The Instant Focus Formula: Cut Through the Noise

The Secret Language of Colors: Unlocking the Emotional Codes

Sacred Fossil Chronicles: Blank Journal

The Christmas Cottage Miracle

Feeding Frenzy: Graboid-Inspired Recipes

Manifest in Minutes: The Quick Law of Attraction Guide

The Symbiote Chronicles: Doctor Who's Venomous Journey

Think Tiny, Grow Big: The Minimalist Mindset

The Energy Key: Unlocking Limitless Motivation

New Year, New Magic: Manifesting Your Best Year Yet

Unstoppable You: Mastering Confidence in Minutes

Infinite Energy: The Secret to Never Feeling Drained

Lightning Focus: Mastering the Art of Productivity in a Distracted World

Saturnalia Manifestation Magick: A Guide to Unlocking Abundance During the Solstice

Graboids and Garland: The Ultimate Tremors-Themed Christmas Guide

12 Nights of Holiday Magic

The Power of Pause: 60-Second Mindfulness Practices

The Quick Reset: How to Reclaim Your Life After Burnout

The Shadow Eater: A Tale of Despair and Survival

The Micro-Mastery Method: Transform Your Skills in Just Minutes a Day

Reclaiming Time: How to Live More by Doing Less
Chronovore: The Eternal Nexus
The Mind Reset: Unlocking Your Inner Peace in a Chaotic World
Confidence Code: Building Unshakable Self-Belief
Baby the Vampire Terrier
Baby the Vampire Terrier's Christmas Adventure
Celestial Streams: The Content Creator's Astrology Manual
The Wealth Whisperer: Unlocking Abundance with Everyday Actions
The Energy Equation: Maximize Your Output Without Burning Out
The Happiness Algorithm: Science-Backed Steps to Joyful Living
Stress-Free Success: Achieving Goals Without Anxiety
Mindful Wealth: The New Blueprint for Financial Freedom
The Festive Flavors of New Year: A Culinary Celebration
The Master's Gambit: Keys of Eternal Power
Shadowed Secrets: Groundhog Day Mysteries
Beneath the Burrow: Lessons from the Groundhog
Spring's Whispers: The Groundhog's Prediction
The Limitless Mindset: Unlock Your Untapped Potential
The Focus Funnel: How to Cut Through Chaos and Get Results
Bold Moves: Building Courage to Live on Your Terms
The Daily Shift: Simple Practices for Lasting Transformation
The Quarter-Life Reset: Thriving in Your 20s and 30s
The Art of Shadowplay: Building Your Own Personal Myth
The Eternal Loop: Finding Purpose in Repetition
Burrowing Wisdom: Life Lessons from the Groundhog
Shadow Work: A Groundhog Day Perspective
Love in Bloom: 5-Minute Romantic Gestures
The Shadowspell Codex: Secrets of Forbidden Magick
The Burnout Cure: Finding Balance in a Busy World
The Groundhog Prophecy: Unlocking Seasonal Secrets
Nog Tales: The Spirited History of Eggnog

Six More Weeks: Embracing Seasonal Transitions
The Lumivian Chronicles: Fragments of the Fifth Dimension
Money on Your Mind: A Beginner's Guide to Wealth
The Focus Fix: Breaking Through Distraction
January's Spirit Keepers: Mystical Protectors of the Cold
Creativity Unchained: Unlocking Your Wildest Ideas in 2025
Manifestation Mastery: 365 Days to Rewrite Your Reality
The Groundhog's Mirror: Reflecting on Change
The Weeping Angels' Christmas Curse
Burrowed in Time: A Groundhog Day Journey
Heartbeats: Poems to Share with Your Valentine
Dino Wicca: The Sacred Grimoire of Prehistoric Magick
Courage of the Pride: Finding Your Inner Roar
The Lion's Leap: Bold Moves for Big Results
Healthy Hustle: Achieving Without Overworking
Practical Manifesting: Turning Dreams into Reality in 2025
Jurassic Pharaohs: Unlocking the Magick of Ancient Egypt and Dino Wicca
The Happiness Equation: Small Changes for Big Joy
The Confidence Compass: Finding Your Inner Strength
Whispers in the Hollow: Tales of the Forgotten Beasts
Echoes from the Hollow: The Return of Forgotten Beasts
The Hollow Ascendant: The Rise of the Forgotten Beasts
The Relationship Reset: Building Better Connections
Mastering the Morning: How to Win the Day Before 8 AM
The Shadow's Dance: Groundhog Day Symbolism
Cupid's Kitchen: Quick Valentine's Day Recipes
Valentine's Day on a Budget: Love Without Breaking the Bank
Astrocraft: Aligning the Stars in the World of Minecraft
Forecasting Life: Groundhog Day Reflections
Bleeding Hearts: Twisted Tales of Valentine's Terror
Herbal Smoke Revolution: The Ultimate Guide to Nature's Cigarette Alternative

Winter's Wrath: The Complete Survival Blueprint for Extreme Freezes.

The Groundhog's Shadow: A Tale of Seasons

Burrowed Insights: Wisdom from the Groundhog

Sensual Strings: The Art of Erotic Bondage

Whispered Flames: Unlocking the Power of Fire Play

Forgotten Shadows: A Guide to Cryptids Lost to Time

Six Weeks of Secrets: Groundhog Day's Hidden Messages

Shadows and Cycles: Groundhog Day Reflections

The Art of Love Letters: Crafting the Perfect Message

Romantic Getaways at Home: Turning Your Space into Paradise

Purrfect Brews: A Cat Lover's Guide to Coffee and Companionship

The Groundhog's Wisdom: Timeless Lessons for Modern Life

The Shadow Oracle: Groundhog Day as a Predictor

Emerging from the Burrow: A Journey of Renewal

The Language of Love: Learning Your Partner's Love Style

Authorpreneur: The Ultimate Blueprint for Writing, Publishing, and Thriving as an Author

Weathering the Seasons: Groundhog Day Perspectives

Valentine's Day Magic: A Guide to Romantic Rituals

The Shadow Chronicles: Stories of Groundhog Day

Love and Laughter: Fun Games for Valentine's Day

AstroRealty: Unlocking the Stars for Property Success

The Groundhog's Path: A Guide to Seasonal Balance

Groundhog Day Diaries: Reflections in the Shadow

The Groundhog's Light: Illuminating the Path Ahead

Valentine's Traditions from Around the World

AI Wealth Revolution: Unlocking the Trillionaire Mindset

Love Rekindled: Reigniting Passion in Relationships

Single and Thriving: Self-Love on Valentine's Day

Emerald Legends: Mystical Tales of Ireland

Green Alchemy: Harnessing Nature's Magic
The Hearts of Horror: A Valentine's Day Nightmare
The Leprechaun's Guide to Wealth and Wisdom
Dancing with the Sidhe: Celebrating the Otherworld
Shamrocks and Shadows: Mysteries of the Green Isle
Emerald Energy: Harnessing Luck and Growth
The Gingerbread Golem's Valentine: A Sweetheart's Guide to Love and Enchantment
The Celtic Knot: Weaving Life and Destiny
Green Fire: Elemental Magic for St. Patrick's Day
Clover Chronicles: Finding Your Inner Luck
Ireland's Mystical Creatures: A Field Guide
Gingerbread Golem's Love Almanac
Prowl and Thrive: The Lion's Guide to Success
Love Alchemy: Transforming Your Life Through Heart Energy
WORLD DOMINATION: Woman's Rule 3:The New Life
The Midnight Rose: A Guide to Lunar Love Spells
The Forbidden Letters: Writing Your Own Love Prophecy
Luck and Lore: St. Patrick's Day for Modern Mystics
The Green Path: A Pagan Celebration of Renewal
The Dark Architect's Guide to Reprogramming Reality
Prankster's Paradise: A Guide to Harmless Hijinks
Manifest Your Reality: The Law of Attraction Simplified
The TARDIS Owner's Manual: Understanding the Doctor's Ship: *A complete guide to the TARDIS, its technology, secrets, and mysteries*
Starlit Romance: Astrology Secrets for Finding True Love
The Time Lord's Atlas: A Complete Guide to the Whoniverse: ***A breakdown of the locations, planets, and dimensions explored in Doctor Who***
Sweetheart Shadows: The Dark Side of Love and Attraction
February Fire: Reigniting Passion in Every Area of Life

The Self-Love Toolkit: 5 Ways to Embrace Who You Are
February Sparks: Ignite Your Dreams in 28 Days
March to Success: A 31-Day Action Blueprint
Ancient Paths: The 13 Sacred Principles of Dino Wicca
Echoes of Tomorrow: Navigating the AI Revolution
The Wellness Blueprint: Balancing Mind, Body, and Soul
Green Horizons: Sustainable Living for a Better Tomorrow
The AI Wealth Code: How to Make Millions with Automation
AI-Powered Creativity: Writing, Art, and Music for Profit
Extinction Rites: Rebirthing Your Soul Through Prehistoric Magick
Sacred Serpents tarot
Celestial Enchantment blank journal
Star Strains
Culinary Journeys: Exploring Global Flavors at Home
The Hollowvale Curse
The Hollowvale Harvest
The Egg of Transformation: Awakening Your Inner Power
Blooming Into Power: A Wiccan Guide to Spring Awakening
The Nightmare Nexus: The Third Doctor's Perilous Haunting
Digital Detox: Reclaiming Your Life in a Connected World
Ostara's Path: Walking the Spiral of Renewal
The Sacred Hare
Financial Freedom: Building Wealth in the Modern Age
Spring's Cauldron: Stirring the Waters of Change
The Hollowvale Pact
Quantum Consciousness: The Science of Reality Shifting
The Hollowvale Hunger
The Sacred Waters Within: A Witch's Guide to Hydrocephalus Magick
The Raven's Nest: Building a Life of Unshakable Stability
AI and the Human Mind: The Future of Intelligence
The Hollowvale Reckoning

Timeless Love: Building and Maintaining Lasting Relationships

The Raven's Roar: Unlocking Unstoppable Confidence

Raven Sight: Awakening Intuition and Inner Wisdom

The Butterfly Effect: Small Changes, Big Transformations

Taming the Boogeyman: How to Conquer Your Inner Fears

The Magick of Green: Awakening Earth's Energy in You

The Entrepreneurial Mindset: Secrets to Business Success

The Hollowvale End

The Shadow Luck Ritual: Reclaiming Power from Your Dark Side

Spring Magick for Beginners: A Simple Guide to Seasonal Energy Work

Doctor Who: The Hollowvale Conundrum

The March of Miracles: Unlocking Synchronicities in Spring

Unveiling the Cosmos: A Guide to Stargazing and Space Exploration

The Ultimate Guide to Surviving an Economic Collapse

The AI Gold Rush: How to Profit from the AI Revolution

Bastet's Shadow: The Hidden Power of Feline Magick

The Bastet Codex: Unlocking the Goddess's Magickal Secrets

Purring Spells: Harnessing Bastet's Healing Frequencies

Bastet's Nine Lives: Rebirth, Transformation, and Immortality Spells

Primal Currents: Hydrocephalus Magick in the Path of Dino Wicca

The Digital Gold Rush: Mastering E-Commerce and Online Sales

Future Shock: Adapting to the Next Decade of Change

The Quantum Mindset: Think Like a Billionaire

Sacred Motherhood: Awakening the Divine Feminine Within

The Mother's Spellbook: Enchantments for Love, Protection, and Prosperity

The Witch's Guide to Parenting: Raising Empowered and Intuitive Children

The Magick of Motherhood: Reclaiming Your Power Through Rituals

The Pagan Path to Self-Love: A Goddess's Guide to Worth and Confidence

Wild Woman Magick: Unleashing Your Primal Power

The Money Magnet Blueprint: Unlocking Unlimited Wealth

Biohacking 101: Unlock Your Body's Full Potential

The Wild Father: A Pagan Guide to Strength and Wisdom

The Sacred Masculine: Unlocking Your Inner Power

The Druid's Compass

The Warrior's Mindset

The Father's Fire

Odin's Path

Ancestral Bonds

The House That Whispers

The Magician's Code

The Wild Hunt

The Green Man's Path

The Altar of Success

The Shadow and the Sword

The High Priestess's Guide to Energy Healing

The Lunar Mother

The Sacred Self-Care Grimoire

The Womb Wisdom Codex

The Wheel of the Mother

The Witch's Guide to Manifestation

The Q2 Reset

The Ultimate Guide to AI-Powered Passive Income

Escape the 9-5

AI Feline Fortunes

The Tear-Stained Grimoire

Razorblade Runes
Cemetery Sirens
The Midnight Wristwatch
The Town That Forgets
AI Horror & Creepypasta
The Hollow Frequency
The Breach Echo
The Quiet Between Worlds
The Sigil of Tharan-Khul
Summon the Vault of Y'ha'ten
The Becoming Codex
The Profit of Az'ra-nar
The Drowned Logos
Echoes of the Eldritch Will
The Deep Ledger
Necronomicon of Networth
Covenant of the Wealthwyrm
The Whisperer's Manifesto
The Rites of Azh-K'luth
The Ark of the Crawling Coin
The Tithe of Shadows
Inkheart Abyss
The Timewinds of Y'ha-nthlei
The Spiral Labyrinth of Azag-Nirrh
The Gallifreyan Heresy of the Black Pharaoh
The Psalms of Nyog-Sotha
Black Rain Alchemy
The Infinite Maw
The Entropic Blueprint
The Oracle of Sh'guul
The Book of Breach
The Drowned Saint's Testament
Dreamcraft of the Sleeper God

The Silence Market
Cthonomics: The Dark Wealth Algorithm
Invocation of the Ten-Eyed King
Wealthbound to the Wyrm Below
Become the Unnameable
Codex of the Sovereign Flame
Rituals of Relentless Becoming
The Shadow Ascends
The Eyes Beneath You
The Will That Wakes Worlds
Silence Is a Weapon
The Mirror That Screams
The Whisper Between Moments
The Mind That Devours Fear
The Myth of the Finished Self
The Architect of Your Madness
The Voice You've Buried
The Discipline of Madness
Stormborn: Awakening Your Inner Tempest
The Mind That Ate Time
Unbind Your Becoming
The Pact You Owe Yourself
The Devourer's Diet
The Acid That Carves the Path
The Tower You Must Burn
The Breath Between Worlds
Speak Like the Deep
The Labyrinth Within
The Spine of the Sea God
Rejection Is a Portal
The Crown You Refused
The Scar Is the Spell
The Lightless Flame

The Habit of Becoming Horrific
ChickenJockey Chaos
The Gatekeeper Within
You Are Not Your Name
The Compass of the Mad
The Archive of Unsent Letters
What the Mirror Can't Show You
The Knife You Needed
Worship Nothing, Become Everything
The Other Voice
The Body the World Forgot
The Vein of the Void
The Black Bone Codex
The Puzzle of the Hidden Self (Millennium Puzzle)
The Eye That Sees the Lie *(Millennium Eye)*
The Ring of Return (Millennium Ring)
The Rod of Relentless Will ***(Millennium Rod)***
The Tally of the Soul (Millennium Tauk/Necklace)
The Key to the Locked Timeline (Millennium Key)
The Scale of Sacred Decisions (Millennium Scales)
Inferno Bites: The UnOfficial Minecraft Lava Cookbook
Rot in the Attic
Prana: The Hidden Force of Your Infinite Self
The Shadow Realm Within: Transforming Darkness Into Destiny
The Borderland Collapse
Claws of Protection: Bastet's Defensive Magick
Mr. Ring-a-Ding's Madness
Yugioh Astrology: Celestial Deckcraft and Duel Destiny (2026–2027 Edition)
The Seal You Signed: Unlocking the Power You Once Feared
The Puzzle of Infinite Minds: Unlocking the Mentalism Hidden Within

The Eye That Mirrors the All: Secrets of Inner Reflection
Doctor Who: The Toymaker's Broadcast
The Rod of Eternal Flow: Commanding the Currents of Vibration
Golden Eyes of Bastet: Enhancing Psychic Vision
The Key of Dual Forces: Balance Within the Polarity
The Scales of Living Rhythm: Timing the Dance of Life
The Necklace of Hidden Cause: Weaving the Webs of Fate
The Ring of Secret Masters: Rising Through the All Within All
Daggers of the Dying Deep
Bastet's Wealth and Fortune Magick: Prosperity Rituals of the Goddess
The Tide that Speaks
The Scrolls of Petosiris: 13 Rituals from the Feathered Eye
Petosiris and the Living Plague of Osirion
Feline Fire: Bastet's Passion and Love Magick
The Star Altar of Petosiris
Bastet's Whiskers: Supernatural Sensory Magick
The Bastet Grimoire
Feeding the Shadows
The Mouthless Prayer
The Spiral Wound
Becoming the Ibis: Lessons from Petosiris's Mind
The Crimson Coven: Cola Magick for Sweet Dominion
Sacred Cat's Paw
The Soda Zodiac: A Flavor for Every Sign
Covenant of the Crawling Flame
The Ink of Ish'Zur
Frothroot: The Thirst That Ate the World
The Golden Glyphs of Prosperity
The Etherbind Codex
Echoes of the Resistance: Reclaiming the You That Survived

Harnessed Minds: Breaking Free from Mental Control
The Eyes in the Smoke
Rootwake: The Carbon Covenant
Skitter Logic: Unlearning the Fear That Built You
Doctor Who: The World That Froths
Rootwake: The Fizz That Rewrites Flesh
Rootwake: Frothfather of the World
The Holly Pact: Blood Beneath the Mistletoe
The 2nd Mass Principle: Building Unbreakable Tribes
Web of Wits: A Survival Guide to Encounters with Anasi the Spider (Aunt Nancy)
The Hexbreaking Handbook: Effective Spells to Remove Curses
Pop Alchemy: Transform Your Life One Sip at a Time
The Mason Code: Leading in Unleadable Times
Petosiris and the Fifth Chamber of Thoth
The Ether Seed Within
The Parent of Tomorrow
Petosiris's Pyramid of Perpetual Wealth
Unlearn the World
Grimoire of the Hollow Tongue
Zodiac Weeds: Finding Your Strain Through the Stars
Aquarius Rises in the Bank
The Sugar God's Smile
The Skinclock Reversal: Biohacking the Face of Time
Debtburn: How to Obliterate What You Owe Forever
The Ice Cream Oracle: What Your Cone Says About Your Future
Silence Is Sovereignty: The Power of Being Unreadable
The Wind That Whispers Through Stone
Path of the Four Directions
Doctor Who: The Maestro's Symphony of Endings
Oxygen Grail: Breathing to Undo the Clock

Zodiacal Collapse: When Stars Devour Time
Teachings from the Red Sand Silence
Doctor Who: Omega – The Broken Equation
Memory Wipe Your Past: Start Over Like a MiB
Mitochondria Prime: Ignite the Core of Youth
A Nest of Roaches
Grub from the Galaxy: MiB Recipes You'll Never Forget
Whiskers of Power: Bastet's Guide to Inner Sovereignty
The Gift Must Cost Them: Negotiation Through Unequal Exchange
The Worm Guys' Wealth Code: Hustle Like an Alien
Bug Out: The Edgar Method for Ruthless Goal Setting
Weaving Life with Spiderwoman's Pattern
Doctor Who: The Rani's Renaissance
How to Get a Job (If You're a Puppygirl)
Speak Through Others: The Art of Proxy Power
T-Rex Your Trauma: Reclaim the Power of Your Primal Self
The Black Briefcase: How MiB Stay Wealthy in Silence
The Thirst Beyond Reason: Understanding Diabetes Insipidus From the Inside Out
Backwoods Witchcraft for Billionaires: The Pagan Path from Dirt Roads to Gold Roads
The Moonshine Grimoire: Fermented Spells for Abundance
The Nameless Geometry
The Wraith's Mixtape: Spellcasting with Songs of Sorrow
The Gallifreyan Gentleman: Silent Wealth, Sonic Confidence, and the Doctor's Code of Living
Sugar Water Confidence
Dino Totems: Spirit Guides from Earth's First Gods
Pumpkin Sigils & Ritual Smoke
The Hózhó Compass
The Distortus Discipline – Order from Inner Mutation
Witchcraft for the Cold-Blooded Soul

Moonlight Over the Blessingway
Water, Interrupted: When the Body Forgets How to Hold On
Deformed but Divine: Embracing Your Asymmetry
Hexes in the Henhouse: The Farm Witch's Guide to Power
The Reversed Flame: A Grimoire of Inverted Power
Salt, Cells, and Sanity: Reclaiming Balance with Diabetes Insipidus
King of the Broken: Crowning the Flawed Self
Moonlight Scars: Emo Moon Magick and the Art of Lunar Sorrow
Noose Spells: Magick of the Hanging Rope
The Goth Cathedral: Rituals of the Broken and Beautiful
The Cretaceous Codex: Dino Spirits and Fossil Magick
The Turkey Bones Ritual
Nine Lives of Manifestation: Unlocking Bastet's Reality Codes
Chaos Muscles: Building Strength from Twisted Pain
Emo Blood Magick: The Veins of Power
The 3AM Flood: Nighttime Urination, Sleep Loss, and the DI Spiral
The Silence Between the Stars
The Lemon Method: Sour Your Way to Success
Starlit Sovereign
The Rite of Twelve Gates: Walking the Gates of the Duat.
Cornbread and Conjure: Recipes for Riches and Rootwork
The Black Rose Rituals: Emo Love Spells and Obsession Magick
The Eternal Goodbye: Death Magick and Rebirth Rituals
Sinkrot: The Drain That Remembers
The Hybrid Mindset: Thinking Beyond Evolution
Bone Dry: Navigating Dehydration Before It Breaks You
Wreathcraft: Winter Sigils and Yuletide Spells
The Rite of Twelve Mouths

S'mores of the Damned: Haunted Recipes for Halloween Night

Rethink the Drink: A Beverage Survival Guide for DI Warriors

The Shadow Chord: Guitar Magick and Sonic

Malformed Yet Majestic: Leading When You Feel Wrong Inside

The Cursed Diary: Ink-Stained Spells of the Emo Soul

Anxiety Off Switch: Emergency Reset for a Fried Nervous System

The Energy Heist: How to Take Back Your Life from Drainers

Beyond the Bathroom: Rebuilding Your Social Life With DI

Coyote's Gift for Decision Makers

Ghoul-Goo: Spooky S'mores You'll Die For

Echoes in the Mirror: Scrying and Self-Destruction Magick

Thread and Thorn: Stitching Spells from Rural Cloth

The Mogwai Mind: Building Untouchable Wealth from Small Ideas

Be Your Own Guide: Trust Your Inner Compass

Hormones in Chaos: The Endocrine Puzzle of Diabetes Insipidus

ChronoCleanse: Detox Your Biological Timeline

The Limb You Hide Is the One That Saves You

Leaves, Bones, and Whisper Spells

The Dinosaur Mindset: Prehistoric Tactics for Modern Wealth

Clawing Back Control: A Bastet Method for Boundaries and Empowerment

Samhain Codes of the Forgotten

Orange Alchemy: The Autumnal Spellbook

Monster Within, Master Without

The Sigil That Sleeps

Hearthcraft: Yule Hearth Sigils and Winter Warmth Spells

Temple of the Purring Moon: Rituals from Bastet's Lineage
When the Earth Remembers Your Footsteps
Food for Mood: Eat to Heal Depression, Not Just Survive It
Witch of the Kudzu Vine: Southern Pagan Wealth Secrets
The Invisible Diagnosis: Advocating for Yourself With DI
The Coffin's Lullaby: Sleep Magick and Nightmares as Portals
Ashes of the Will: Rituals for Erasing the Self
The Fracture Rite: Shattering the Magickal Core
Funeral Candles: The Art of Emo Flame Magick
The Black Grimoire: A Blank Ritual for Writing in Absence
Phantom Thirst: A Halloween Survival Guide for Diabetes Insipidus
The Hollow Crown: Emo Royalty and Magick of the Outcast King
Sandpainting for the Soul
Falling Into Balance: Using the Extra Hour to Recalibrate Life
100 Southern Superstitions That Still Work
The DI Child: A Parent's Guide to Raising Hydrated, Happy Kids
The Jungle of Shame: Escaping the Hidden Lab of Doubt
The Witch's Toast: S'mores Spells and Creepy Confections
The Hoodoo Pantry: Spells from the Mason Jar
The Immortal Fortune: Secret Wealth Lessons from Captain Jack Harkness
The Specter's Embrace: Magick for Channeling Ghostly Lovers
Grateful Waters: A Thanksgiving Survival Guide for Diabetes Insipidus
The Seizure Gospel
Harvestbind: Autumn Sigils and Samhain Spells
Doctor Who: The Algorithmic Awakening
Silent Nights, Steady Waters: A Christmas Survival Guide for Diabetes Insipidus

The Extra Hour Effect: How One Hour Can Transform Everything

Blade Between the Breaths

Running with the Mountain Shadows

Echoes of the Failed Experiment – Becoming a Living Legacy

Swamp Witches & River Ghosts: Real Southern Hauntings

Cornbread Prophecies: Magical Recipes from a Southern Table

Doctor Who: The Signal in the Star

Bloomcraft: Spring Sigils and Equinox Enchantments

Vanisher: How to Disappear from the Internet Without Losing Your Life

The Ultimate Christmas Cookie Cookbook

The Unbreakable Parent: How to Mentally Survive Raising Kids in a Broken World

Time Debt: How to Reclaim the Hours You Didn't Know You Lost

One Month, One Million: Unconventional Cash Creation Tactics

Doctor Who: The Cyber Conversion Protocol

Black Friday Frenzy: The Art of Finding Hidden Online Deals

The Grimoire Buried Under the Apple Tree

Digital Couponing Masterclass: Your Step-by-Step Guide to Black Friday Savings

The Fire Inside the Flint

Shadows on the Ceiling: The Emo Guide to Astral Magick

The Bone-Eaters Beneath Us

Black Friday Bundle Blueprint: Creating Irresistible Product Packages for Maximum Sales

Thirteen Nights of Unbinding

Doctor Who: Engines of Influence

Pumpkin Spice Alchemy: Recipes of Fire and Frost

When Raptor Met Rexy: Prehistoric Lessons in Wild Romance

Oblivion's Candle: Burn the Path Behind You

Campfire Curses and Chocolate: A Halloween S'mores Grimoire

The Wallet That Wasn't Mine: Breaking Free from Inherited Scarcity

The Cola Zodiac: What Your Fizz Says About Your Fate

Frostfire Fortune: Unlocking Winter's Hidden Prosperity

Signal Jamming: Detox Your Brain from Info Overload

The Dust of the Forgotten Rite

The Golden Cat Sigils: Drawing Power in Bastet's Name

Mud Magick: The Prosperity of Getting Dirty

Savory Spicefall: Beyond the Pumpkin Pie

Pumpkin Spice Apothecary Kitchen

The Pumpkin Spice Economy: Turning Trends into Billions

The Ember Veil: 13 Nights of Fire Magick

Financial Freeze: When Earning Triggers Panic

The Gingerbread Alchemist: Sweet Recipes with a Twist

Biosynth Power: Programming Yourself from Scratch

Echoes from the Talking Circle

Truffle Alchemy: Fungus of Fortune

Spores of Power: The Truffle Witch's Handbook

Doctor Who: The Tower That Speaks

The Mycelium Veil: Truffle Magick Unbound

Broke But Ashamed: Healing the Shame Wound of Debt

The Evergreen Mind: Growth Through Winter Stillness

The Black Veil Truffle Rite

The Voice Beneath Symbols

Witchlight on the Bayou: Swamp Spells for Sovereignty

I Grew Up Poor and Now I Sabotage My Success

The Lantern of Hollow Souls

Shutdown Survival: A Citizen's Guide to Thriving When Government Stops

When Abundance Feels Like a Threat: Healing the Hidden Fears of Enough

The Scarecrow Grimoire

Owls of the October Veil

Candlewax and Curses: A Halloween Spellbook

Excavating the Inner Fossil – Transforming Fossilized Thoughtforms into Tools of Power

The Yule Witch's Spellbook: Magick for the Holiday Season

Haunted Christmas: Ghost Stories for Winter Nights

The Christmas Survival Guide: Thriving Through the Chaos

The Bone Orchard Rites

Haunted Commerce: The Ghost in the Marketplace

Get Some Tarot cards: https://www.makeplayingcards.com/sell/apophis-occult-shop

Get some shirts: https://www.bonfire.com/store/apophis-shirt-emporium/

Instagrams:
@apophis_enterprises,
@apophisbookemporium,
@apophisscardshop
Twitter: @apophisenterpr1
Tiktok:@apophisenterprise
Youtube: @sg1fan23477
Hive: @sg1fan23477
CheeLee: @SG1fan23477

Podcast: Apophis Chat Zone: https://open.spotify.com/show/5zXbrCLEV2xzCp8ybrfHsk?si=fb4d4fdbdce44dec

Newsletter: https://apophiss-newsletter-27c897.beehiiv.com/

If you want to support me or see posts of other projects that I have come over to: **buymeacoffee.com/mpetchinskg**

I post there daily several times a day

Get your Dinowicca or Christmas themed digital products, especially Santa Raptor songs and other musics. Here: **https://sg1fan23477.gumroad.com**

Apophis Yuletide Digital has not only digital Christmas items, but it will have all things with Dinowicca as well as other Digital products.

www.ingramcontent.com/pod-product-compliance
Lightning Source LLC
LaVergne TN
LVHW022221200926
848481LV00006B/2059
* 9 7 9 8 3 4 9 6 0 7 2 7 1 *